Jesus and Justice

Organizing for God's Reign on Earth
Then and Now

John Dominic Crossan
&
Michael Okinczyc-Cruz

AMNA PRESS
Chicago, Illinois

Cover Design and interior illustrations by Izzy Spitz

ISBN: 979-8-218-89199-2

INTRODUCTION

The life of the historical Jesus is a revolutionary story. Yet, when it comes to revolutionary stories that challenge the status quo, they are often buried or sugarcoated by powerful people and institutions. Revolutionary stories generate memories that are perceived as dangerous for some and a source of inspiration for others. Revolutionary stories are provocative. They stir the waters. They unsettle the comfortable. They comfort the afflicted. They pierce through the layers of deception and double-dealing that the ultra wealthy and powerful stand upon.

Most importantly, revolutionary stories give birth and rise to future revolutionaries by planting seeds of courage and imagination in the hearts, minds and spirits of God's beloved – those who have been discarded by the mighty. Without the telling of revolutionary stories and in the absence of revolutionary memories, we are unable to perceive and fully participate as co-creators in God's unfolding vision and plan.

Through the lives of Miriam and Moses, Mary and Jesus, God boldly proclaimed justice, love, righteousness and freedom from bondage as cornerstones of God's hope for this world. Proclaiming this vision within the context of Pharaoh's Egypt and the Roman Empire marked Moses and Miriam, Jesus and Mary, as revolutionaries. We know from the Old Testament story of the Exodus that Moses and the Israelites engaged in a profoundly risky and daunting confrontation with Pharaoh's Egyptian empire and its ruthless slave labor economy of production. Without God's divine intervention and relentless prodding of Moses to act, the Israelites would not have rejected Pharaoh's imperialistic economy and its physical, psychological, and spiritual grip over their lives. Similarly, Jesus and his movement of poor and destitute peasants and workers embarked on a nonviolent confrontation with the Roman Empire's economy of domination and extractive exploitation.

As Jesus observed and discerned over 2,000 years ago during a time of profound conflict and oppression, we find ourselves today at a moral crossroads. The modern day political, economic, military and social forces that shape our daily lives regard billions of people and Mother Earth as objects for exploitation and extraction. Companies such as Exxon, Amazon, Walmart, Google, Meta, Lockheed Martin and Blackstone operate ruthlessly on a global scale. International corporations and powerful nations, business titans and politicians, conspire, cooperate, and commiserate to maximize profits and returns.

Pope Francis referred to this arrangement as *corporate colonialism*. God's planet and the ample resources it offers are held in bondage by corporate and political forces that prioritize greed and profit over the Common Good. Troublingly, our lives today are deeply intertwined with the consumerist culture that corporations relentlessly promote. Our addiction to consumer goods (wealth, entertainment and products) rather than to spiritual goods (nature, human connection and contemplation) is a dynamic that corporations are quite eager to continue to shape and influence. As a result, the delicate fabric of human life and our ecosystems are rapidly fraying and being destroyed. The fragile and vulnerable state of our communities and Mother Earth has not solely produced a political and economic crisis, but a deep spiritual crisis as well. Our present socio-economic arrangements and spiritual conditions are scandalous to God.

We are in desperate need of a revolution of values and of our political and economic systems today. Nothing short of a revolution of love with justice as its aim to addresses the foundational systems and ideologies that produce inequality and suffering is required. What this involves is a deep personal and spiritual conversion within those who respond to God's call to be protagonists for God's Reign on Earth.

Revolutions of this type have emerged before. Mahatma Gandhi, Rigoberta Menchú, Rev. Dr. Martin Luther King Jr., Dolores Huerta and Dorothy Day were all inspired by the life and teachings of Jesus to organize and lead nonviolent movements within their respective time and place. This is precisely why the story of the historical Jesus, a first-century Galilean Jew who emerged into a world of desperate existence, ruthless exploitation and Roman imperial domination, is vitally important to tell. Amidst the depths of violence, despair and hopelessness that were pervasive during his time, Jesus led a nonviolent movement that boldly challenged the reign of the powerful and mighty political, economic and religious forces against which he proclaimed God's Reign on Earth. The story of the historical Jesus is a story that we believe many elders, parents, students, churchgoers, workers, organizers, activists and everyday people are eager to hear.

Who Needs To Hear the Story of the Revolutionary Jesus

We worshipped Jesus instead of following him on his same path. We made Jesus into a mere religion instead of a journey toward union with God and everything else. This shift made us into a religion of "belonging and believing" instead of a religion of transformation.
- Richard Rohr

Several months before the pandemic struck, a group of undergraduate university students gathered to participate in a training about faith-rooted community organizing and the historical Jesus. Towards the end of training, one of the students shared her reflections from the day: "*I never knew that Jesus, Mary and Joseph were refugees, impoverished and exploited. This was never taught to me before in Church.*" Earlier that day, this student had spent several hours with her peers learning about the tools, methodologies and practices of faith-rooted community organizing and the nonviolent movement of poor and dispossessed people Jesus had led.

The training that day, facilitated by the Coalition for Spiritual and Public Leadership (CSPL), was not an ordinary classroom discussion. Students gathered in small groups and read excerpts from John Dominic

Crossan's writings about Jesus' social, political and economic context. Through a popular education pedagogy, these students reflected critically on the materials and made brilliant connections between the socio-economic challenges that Jesus faced as a first-century Galilean Jew who lived under Roman imperial occupation and many of the challenges that they and their families face living within the United States. Many of these students, through their own working-class backgrounds and their experiences as immigrants or children of immigrants, could relate to the struggles that Jesus and his people faced as peasants and noncitizens in their own land. Others felt that they could empathize with what it meant to live in a community and society that was heavily militarized and shaped by constant surveillance carried out by state and federal authorities.

For Jesus, life was profoundly shaped by the terrifying presence of Roman military troops that swiftly and violently suppressed any form of protest against the injustices they endured daily. For many of these students, they were keenly aware of the conscious and unconscious depths of fear, intimidation and anxiety that the constant threat of police violence or immigration enforcement produces in their families and communities. When it came to reading about the economic conditions that Jesus and his people faced, this group of students made immediate connections between the struggles of first-century peasant farmers, day laborers, fishermen, servants and the economic pressures and forms of economic exploitation that they and their families similarly face from working in factories or as gig workers.

This story is one of several moments where our respective work in the fields of biblical scholarship and faith-rooted community organizing has come together. We believe that the revolutionary story of the historical Jesus must be broadly shared with people from all walks of life and critically engaged by Christians and followers of Jesus in their assessment and judgment of our present day socio-economic challenges and crises. Martin Luther King Jr., Rigoberta Menchú, Dolores Huerta, and countless others have put their faith into practice by engaging deeply with Jesus' teachings and the biblical texts. Through this critical engagement, they sought to discern the signs of the times and respond to God's call to build a more loving and just world. The same is not only possible today, but is urgently necessary.

The type of historically rooted biblical interpretation, theological reflection and critical socio-economic analysis that these students engaged in is a vitally important practice that we must broaden and expand within faith communities and within circles of faith-rooted community organizing. Fostering a depth of historical biblical knowledge is essential if we are to meaningfully engage scripture and Jesus' teachings in our moral examination of contemporary socio-economic affairs. The renowned Swiss theologian Karl Barth once said that Christians are to "Keep the Bible in one hand, and the newspaper in the other." Barth lived during the 1930's when Nazi ideology and its alignment with the Christian movement in Germany was on the rise. The rise of Christian nationalism, unbridled capitalism, the degradation of Mother Earth, and war and genocide in our world today is an urgent spiritual and political crisis that people of faith and moral conviction must respond to collectively and nonviolently. For far too long, Christians of all different traditions and denominations have failed to contend with theological convictions and beliefs that are false and hateful.

Nurturing a deeper knowledge of the revolutionary story of Jesus and the historical context of his life is vitally important. However, we recognize that intellectual knowledge alone without concerted, organized and sustained commitment, action, and grassroots power does not foster fundamental societal change. If we want to build a world that is more just, equitable and compassionate, we must *follow* Jesus' teachings and example. This work also involves the inner spiritual development and conversion that opens our hearts and minds to God's love and grace and the movements of the Holy Spirit.

While there is a great deal of worshiping of Jesus going on in the world, there are not nearly enough people who are *following* Jesus. Is it easy and simple to do? *Certainly not.* We can begin by learning about the first-century Mediterranean world under Roman occupation as Jesus experienced it and apply what we learn to our present spiritual and socio-economic challenges. Over the course of this book, we will explore the following themes outlined in each of the three chapters: *The Vision of Jesus, The Execution of Jesus, and The Resurrection of Jesus.*

While each chapter will provide scholarly matrix for the historical Jesus in light of the religious, political and socio-economic context that shaped his vision, message, and actions, this research is also intended to offer a spiritual, theological and sociological point of reference from which we can engage in contemporary analysis and critical reflection of our own political and socio-economic inequalities and systemic challenges today. Over the course of the book, we will talk about *tradition* and its relationship to social movements, beginning with the revolutionary first-century nonviolence movement Jesus founded and led, and social movements today.

Telling the story of the revolutionary Jesus is about reviving a vital part of the liberative Christian tradition that has been obscured by harmful theology and legalistic dogma, and Church hierarchy. We believe the historical Jesus has much to offer to organizers, activists, unionists, workers, students, parishioners and people of faith who are moved by the Spirit, who thirst for justice, and who feel called to make a constructive contribution to the Common Good.

This belief was further clarified and affirmed over the summer of 2024 at the Coalition for Spiritual and Public Leadership's 3-day Congress where John Dominic Crossan, affectionately referred to as Dom, offered a three-part lecture based on the main theme of each chapter. This multiracial, multigenerational and multilingual gathering of over one hundred and fifty grassroots faith-leaders and organizers from across Chicago and the Midwest deepened our conviction that the historical Jesus is a source of profound inspiration and guidance for those whom Pope Francis called *protagonists* and *social poets*. This book is a written testament to what we witnessed and observed over the course of those three days.

We trust that this book will awaken and stir in your hearts and spirits a new dimension to Jesus that will hopefully echo in your prayer lives and work for God's Reign on Earth.

With fervent spirit,

John Dominic Crossan & Michael Okinczyc-Cruz

CHAPTER 1

THE VISION OF JESUS

The love of possessions is a disease in them. These people have made many rules that the rich may break, but the poor may not! They have a religion in which the poor worship, but the rich will not! They even take tithes from the poor and weak to support the rich and those who rule. They claim this mother of ours, the earth, for their own use, and fence their neighbor away. ...
If America had been twice the size it is, there still would not have been enough.
– Sitting Bull

These poignant words from Sitting Bull, the Hunkpapa Lakota leader, reflect his insight into the devastating ideological, political, and economic nature of U.S. colonization efforts across lands during the 18th and 19th centuries that for generations were inhabited by Native American tribes. Born sometime between 1831 and 1837 in the Dakota territory, Sitting Bull's life during the 19th century was dramatically shaped by U.S. political, economic, and military policies that led to the vast colonization and rapid commercialization of Native lands.

Vast amounts of lush and beautiful plains, rivers and mountains were violently seized and stolen by the U.S. government, colonial settlers, and venture capitalists. The Dakota lands that Sitting Bull's Hunkpapa Lakota tribe relied upon for generations were indelibly linked to their spirituality, view of the world, and way of life. The rapid and ruthless commercialization of the plains, rivers, mountains and the living beings that inhabited these territories would dramatically alter this landscape forever. It was this catastrophic situation of systemic commercialization, exploitation, and disregard for the sanctity of God's creation that Sitting Bull's words directly addressed.

What does any of this have to do with the historical Jesus? As it turns out, Jesus' public ministry directly challenged the relentless plundering, exploitation, and heavy taxation that his people were subjected to by the Roman Empire and its local collaborators across Galilee and Judea. Many years and generations prior to the resistance that Sitting Bull and other Native tribes asserted in response to the colonization and commercialization of their lands, a profound drama had unfolded along the shores of the Sea of Galilee in the first century. What was once a public lake that Jews and other first-century Mediterranean peoples relied upon for food and their way of life was transformed into a privatized imperial enterprise.

Herod Antipas viewed the Sea of Galilee and the vulnerable people that lived along its shores as objects for production that could be mercilessly exploited for profit and gain. Sitting Bull and Jesus were both galvanizing historical figures who courageously resisted imperial oppression and the colonization and commercialization of common lands. However, what makes Jesus' movement revelatory is not the elements that he shares in common with other historical revolutionaries, but the way in which his enduring vision, message and path is unique and distinct. As we will explore, Jesus' nonviolent Reign of God movement and vision dramatically expanded and grew along the same shores where Herod Antipas' project of rapid commercialization was unfolding.

HOW DID TRADITION GET TRACTION IN GALILEE? STARTING WITH QUESTIONS

Think about *time*. Why did Jesus happen when he happened? Why in the 20s of that first Common Era century? What if Jesus had happened 50 years earlier as Herod the Great, the Rome-appointed "King of the Jews," was beginning the forcible Romanization of his homeland? What if Jesus had happened 50 years later as his homeland was rising in colonial rebellion against that imperial Romanization? In either case, would Jesus' public life have lasted more than ten minutes. *A vision's time is its destiny.*

Think about *place*—but bring *time* with you. Why did Jesus happen where he happened? Why around the northwest quadrant of the "Sea of Galilee" just as it was becoming the "Sea of Tiberias" (John 6:1; 21:1)? How, in the 20s CE, did a "sea" or lake that was once "of" a province like Galilee, become "of" a city like Tiberias? What was Herod Antipas, son of the late and unlamented Herod the Great, doing as Rome-appointed ruler of Galilee with that lake and that city in the 20s CE? *A vision's place is also its destiny.*

Think about *matrix*. We speak of text *and* context or of foreground *and* background. We use those doubled terms but all too easily, especially in biblical readings, those second terms, context or background, slip quietly into oblivion. Far too often, the Bible is read and interpreted without any historical context. This is a tragic mistake. To avoid such slippage, we use a single term, *matrix*, for the necessity of always keeping text *and* context, foreground *and* background, interactively together—like front *and* back, heads *and* tails of a coin. (Have you ever seen a single-sided coin?)

If we reflect on this on a personal level, understanding the nuances of when we were born (*time*), where we were raised (*place*) and social, economic and political realities both before (*foreground*) and during (*background*) our lifetime matters a great deal in understanding and interpreting our lives. The lives and impact of important historical figures such as Abraham Lincoln or Harriet Tubman cannot be properly understood outside of their historical context, and the same is true for Jesus. Lincoln and Tubman's legacies are inextricably bound to the struggle to abolish the evil institution of slavery in the United States.

The story of the Montgomery bus boycott is a more contemporary example of the importance of interpreting historical figures and movements through the matrix of time and place. Why did the boycott take place when it did (*time*) and where it did (*place*)? What social, political, economic, and historical factors prompted the decision to organize the boycott (*background and foreground*)? While the Montgomery bus boycott officially began in December of 1955, many layers of racial, economic, and political oppression over hundreds of years precipitated this monumental event in the historical arc of the Civil Rights Movement.

While historical context is essential to our understanding of historical figures and movements, we have rarely sought to understand Jesus' historical context in our study and exploration of his life, teachings, and vision. Therefore, *matrix* is essential to understanding how the *text* and *foreground* of the historical Jesus interacts necessarily with the *context* and *background* of the Sea of Galilee, known today as Lake Kinneret, the lake shaped like a harp.

In the following sections, we will explore the ultimate matrix and interaction of Jesus and Herod Antipas by the Sea of Galilee as it was becoming the Sea of Tiberias in the 20s CE. Then we will go deeper into detail about the why and where of Jesus by unpacking how two religio-political and socio-economic movements - the Jordan-Baptism Movement of John and the Reign of God Movement of Jesus occurred in the territory of Herod Antipas in the 20s. What did Herod Antipas do to provoke opposition from both John the Baptist and Jesus of Nazareth?

Finally, it is time to meet and question the one the Romans called *Pater Patriae*, the Father of the Fatherland, and would have thought of himself, in our terms here, as the *Master of the Matrix*.

ENTER CAESAR THE AUGUSTUS

Born as Gaius Octavius in 63 BCE, he was adopted as *son* by his great-uncle Julius Caesar and renamed Gaius Julius Caesar in 44 BCE. Julius Caesar was assassinated by a group of Roman senators, including Brutus and Cassius, in the year 44 BCE because they feared he was becoming too powerful. Following his death, Julius Caesar's identity became "divine" and he "ascended" among the Gods. That adopted son, Gaius Octavius (Caesar Augustus) became, in Latin, *Divi Filius* or Son of the Divine One and, in Greek, *Theou Huios*, or Son of God.

Next, in 31 BCE, by his naval victory over Antony and Cleopatra off the western coast of Greece, Gaius Octavius ended twenty years of savage on-again, off-again civil war that had threatened the very survival of the Roman Empire. After that imperial salvation, his official and bilingual titles started to multiply. He became *Imperator* or *Autokrator*, not just Emperor of the (Roman) Empire but Conqueror of the (Roman) World. He became *Augustus* or *Sebastos*, not just the One to be revered but the One to be *worshipped*. Finally, in poems and cameos, coins and inscriptions, altars and temples, Caesar the Augustus was proclaimed as God, Son of God, God

Incarnate, God from God, Savior of the World, Redeemer from Sin, and Creator of a New World. Sound familiar?

By claiming these titles, Caesar Augustus' reign as the first emperor of Rome could be explained not simply in secular political terms, but also theologically as a divine manifestation of God's will. When rulers, despots, and authoritarians ascend it is most often by securing enough political, economic and military resources to grasp their position of power. Once in power or along the path to securing their power, rulers will often align themselves with key religious figures and institutions that are willing to falsely sanctify their reign as divinely ordained by God.

By doing this, they mobilize ideological power which can be weaponized and leveraged to reinforce whatever corrupt arrangement of unjust political, economic, and military power that they have put in place to serve the interests of a powerful and wealthy minority. While Caesar Augustus' rule over the Roman Empire was secured politically and militarily, it was essential that his reign as Rome's first emperor take on religious and ideological significance both domestically and across Rome's expansive territories to further justify his reign over his subjects. This was something that conquered and colonized first-century Galilean Jews were forced to contend with prior to Jesus' birth and during his lifetime.

The political ascent of Donald Trump beginning in 2015 as a centrally important figure within the Christian nationalist movement is a more contemporary example of an authoritarian political figure who has been consecrated as a preordained leader who has been chosen by God to redeem the United States and return it to its past "strength and glory." During a 2023 interview on Fox News, actor Jim Caviezel who played Jesus in *The Passion of the Christ* referred to Trump as "the new Moses." The alignment between Donald Trump and the Christian nationalist movement and his divinization within that movement is a pressing reality that Christians are challenged to address.

At this stage, there is clearly a question beyond, beneath, or behind Caesar Augustus' adopted titles and proclaimed divinity. Before Jesus ever existed, and even if Jesus had never existed, there already was in that first-century Mediterranean world a human being suffused with the titles of God, Son of God, God Incarnate, Savior of the World and other attributes of divinity. Here, then, is our fundamental question. What did it mean, what could it mean, when all those titles of the imperial ruler, Caesar the Augustus/Sebastos, who lived on the Palatine Hill in Rome were transferred to a Jewish peasant, Jesus the Messiah/Christ, who lived on the Nazareth Ridge in Galilee?

By referring to Jesus as Son of God, God Incarnate and Savior of the World, Jesus' followers were making theological claims that were undeniably anti-imperial. Imagine during his lifetime that Jesus, a poor Jewish peasant, would be endowed with the same titles that Emperor Augustus held during his life and after his death. It served as a bold and defiant message to the Roman Empire! It would have been considered an act of rebellion, treason, and a direct challenge to Rome's ideological claims.

Today we often interpret Jesus' titles as Son of God, God Incarnate, Savior of the World in strictly religious terms. However, during Jesus' lifetime and in the period following his public execution, referring to Jesus in these terms was politically and theologically explosive. These titles held both theological *and* political significance. The message and vision of the Reign of God movement and Jesus' role within it as the Savior of the World was indeed provocative, rebellious, and revolutionary.

AUGUSTUS MAKES A DECISION

One of the ways Rome maintained control and domination across their imperial territories was through a political system of appointing rulers who belonged to the colonized territories to govern their land on behalf of the Roman Empire. This system was established in order to ensure that a ruler who understood the local customs, culture and religion of the people was in place as a form of pacification. Establishing a client king who ruled over a territory on behalf of the Roman Empire also meant that Rome did not have to send as many troops or extend as much political, military or economic capital in order to govern one of its conquered territories. Client kings often secured their position by expressing their devout fealty to the Roman Empire and ensuring a constant flow of taxes and by suppressing any local upheavals to ensure Rome would not lose confidence in their client king's ability to govern and produce for the empire.

Granted all of that, in 4 BCE, Augustus was faced with a crucial decision concerning the Herodian Succession. In March of that year, Herod the Great, Friend of the Romans and King of the Jews, had died in his summer palace at Jericho. During his nearly 30-year appointment, Herod the Great created the port-city of Caesarea, named after Caesar Augustus, to please his Roman masters and expanded the court of the Temple to please his Jewish subjects. Herod the Great did exactly and *more* of what Rome wanted of a client king. He was ruthless, cruel and worked to construct more infrastructure and deliver more power for Rome. Hence, Caesar Augustus was faced with the dilemma of who or what would replace him.

Herod the Great's three eldest sons—by two different wives—had already been executed for treason by 4 BCE. That left three younger sons—by another two wives—as possible successors, subject, of course, to Roman consent. Of the three potential heirs, Herod Antipas was 16, Herod Archelaus 19, and Herod Philip (the Second) was 22 years of age. To help us understand what happened next, we look to Josephus, a Jewish priest-historian.

In his *last* will and testament, Herod proposed to Augustus that none of those three younger sons become "King of the Jews" but that his territories be divided by giving the south to Archelaus, the near north to Antipas, and the far northeast to Philip II. Herod's proposal was clear enough but then a powerful political delegation approached Augustus with alternative proposals equally clear.

That delegation included Herodian family members from Judea, imperial authorities from Syria, and numerous Jewish representatives from both Jerusalem and Rome. Together they offered two strong counter-options to Herod's dying will. Their first request was that Augustus abolish the Herodian Kingdom and establish its territory as an ethnic enclave within the Roman Province of Syria under the authority of its top-level governor. Failing that abolition, their second request was that Antipas—and absolutely not Archelaus—be made "King of the Jews."

The reason for this was because Archelaus had already demonstrated a violent and brutal temperament similar to that of his father. Shortly after Herod the Great's death, Archelaus violently suppressed protests in Jerusalem during Passover by killing 3,000 Jews. This massacre combined with his general lack of experience and fear that he would be another tyrannical leader were key reasons for the organized opposition to his being named "King of the Jews."

Any decision on the Herodian Succession was so important for imperial security on the Mediterranean's Levantine Coast that Augustus convened the high-level delegation in the Temple of Apollo adjacent to his home on the Palatine. In the event, Augustus decided to follow Herod's will by retaining and dividing the kingdom among those three sons. This ensured the Herodian line would continue, which further secured Rome's grip on the Mediterranean's eastern coast. After all, it provided an abundance of agricultural resources, labor, taxes and more. Jesus' people were seen simply as a means to an end and pawns in Rome's broader political, economic, military and ideological ambitions. We can never know for sure what would have happened had Augustus accepted either of those alternative options, but it could hardly have been worse than what eventually happened with the Judeo-Roman War that resulted in the destruction of the Temple in 70 CE.

In reflecting on how Rome imposed its will through compliant local rulers, it becomes clear that the machinery of empire has simply evolved—not disappeared. The mechanisms of control and marginalization seen in Herod's dominions bear unsettling similarities to how global powers operate today. In our modern world, we would like to believe that everyday people can play a vital role in contributing to the major decisions and elections that shape our daily realities and determine who will represent us. This, after all, reflects a cornerstone of what a democratic society and nation should provide to its citizens. Jesus' people had no such role or right. As non-Roman citizens they were a second-class people within their own land. They, therefore, possessed no formal political rights or privileges.

There was no consultation with the poor peasants, day laborers, slaves, masons or carpenters who represented the overwhelming share of the population. This was outside of the realm of possibility within this world in which Roman rulers consulted strictly with other powerful families and figures. Although 2,000 years have passed, we continue to live in a world in which a small number of powerful families, corporations and interest groups determine and shape the political and economic decisions that affect millions of lives.

Just as Augustus and Rome had propped up and empowered Herod the Great and eventually his sons to serve Rome's political, economic, and military interests in that region of the world, U.S. presidents, intelligence agencies and wealthy elite have colluded to do the same throughout the 20th and 21st centuries. For many decades, the United States has played a decisive and devastating role in undermining democratic elections, serving corporate interests, and advancing their own military objectives across Central and South America, the Middle East and other parts of the world. One stark example of this is the U.S. government's support for General Augusto Pinochet's brutal dictatorship in Chile, which came to power through a CIA-backed coup that overthrew the democratically elected president, Salvador Allende, in 1973.

Despite their futile attempts to pacify and suppress their subject populations, empires such as Rome and the United States have always destabilized regions and endlessly produced death and societal instability. The destructive results of the legacy of colonialism, endless wars, political interference, corporate exploitation and the destabilization of the environment has produced catastrophic socio-economic conditions that refugees flee each year. This contextual backdrop of imperial politicking by powerful rulers and wealthy elites was Jesus' reality.

Today there are followers of Jesus who seek to continue pursuing the vision of God's Reign on Earth, which inevitably involves nonviolent confrontations with empires and the ruthless systems of exploitation that empires are built upon. Community organizers are amongst the group who work painstakingly to bring diverse groups together for collective decision making and action to curb the unholy imbalances of power in the world. In this process, organizers establish democratic communities and organizations where decisions that affect the well-being of people and our planet are made by the many and not by the few.

ANTIPAS: THE WOULD-BE "KING OF THE JEWS"

In 4 BCE, Antipas had started his political career as a would-be "King of the Jews," at Rome, under the emperor Augustus. In 39 CE, he would end that career *still* as a would-be "King of the Jews," at Rome, under the emperor Caligula. That first time he had returned not as *monarch* or king but as *tetrarch* (the sovereign or governor of the fourth part of a country). As such, he was prince of Galilee and Perea, two disconnected territories to the west and south of the Sea of Galilee. That last time his failure was worse. Caligula exiled him to Roman Gaul (modern France) and, in his stead, made Herod Agrippa I, "King of the Jews." (We know him from Acts 12.) To be Antipas, was to be ultimately and almost fatally disappointed.

What, however, about Antipas under Tiberius, the emperor in between Augustus and Caligula? To gain favor with emperors, client kings would customarily do lavish things for them in exchange for royal advancement. What, if anything, did Herod Antipas do about royal advancement when Emperor Augustus died in 14 CE? In answer, we do not intend to read his mind but to interpret his action: what did he do factually and how should that be interpreted historically?

On the accession of Tiberius as the new emperor, Antipas could have honored that imperial elevation by building, say a theater, a bath, a stadium, or a triumphal arch in his capital at Sepphoris (known as modern Saffuriya in Arabic and Tzipori in Hebrew), about four miles northwest of Nazareth. He could even have changed the name of that capital from Sepphoris to Tiberias. Instead, Herod Antipas left inland Sepphoris and created a new lakeside capital named Tiberias. That raises a question all too often unasked by Christians: *Why?*

You always need a very good reason to move your capital because that would displease Gods and Goddesses with unattended temples, courtiers and aristocrats with empty mansions, and scribes and artisans with lost opportunities. No wonder, then, that Josephus, the Jewish historian, reports rumors about Tiberias as externally constructed atop a graveyard and internally adorned with forbidden images. Take that, Antipas—and Tiberias! So, to repeat: What very strong reason made Herod Antipas honor the new emperor by relocating his capital; and, granted capital relocation, why move it from a healthy windswept hillock to an unhealthy mosquito-ridden lakeshore?

Our interpretation and proposal is that Antipas was making the second of his three moves to become "King of the Jews," the original title of his late father, Herod the Great. As earlier under Augustus and later under Caligula, so now under Tiberius, Antipas was as always the prince who would be king. But once again, how did a new capital city on the mid-western shore of the Sea of Galilee as it became, thereby, the Sea of Tiberias, fit with that intention?

If Antipas could vastly increase his Galilean tribute, those Roman masters might wonder what he might do if he ruled the whole country as its king. But Antipas could not vastly increase his *tribute* to Rome by squeezing more grain from his peasants without risking a rebellion—the fastest way to become an ex-tetrarch. *But he could vastly expand his land-produce by adding lake-produce to it.* Antipas was interested in accumulating more resources and power at the expense of the poor fishermen and peasants.

The Sea of Galilee and the poor families and villagers that surrounded the lake were seen not as sacred and divine, but as objects for ruthless exploitation. Antipas viewed the Sea of Galilee and his subjects along the lake as a vital linchpin in his political and economic scheme to consolidate power across the territories he desired within the Roman Empire. All of this spelled profound trouble for those poor peasant families who lived along and near to those shores.

There was only one thing the Antipas' lake had that Antipas' land did not: *fish* and thence fish-factories that could deliver dried fish, salted fish, and fish-sauce (*garum*) straight to coastal Tyre and into the imperial commerce of Mediterranean globalization. By 20 CE, then, Tiberias was open for business and that business was controlling the lake, exploiting its fish, and so increasing Antipas' imperial tribute in Galilee so that Tiberius— he hoped—might extend his rule to the whole country as, finally, "King of the Jews."

On the one hand, Antipas' first-minted coins celebrated the foundation of Tiberias with coinage from the "year 24" of his rule, dating from 4 BCE. Those coins omitted any human figures or faces out of respect for his Jewish subjects. On the back or reverse was the two-line word TIBE/RIAS, in Greek, surrounded by a wreath and on the front or reverse was OF HEROD TETRARCH, also in Greek, around a centrally poised reed. That *reed* was chosen to celebrate the lakeside location of Tiberias.

On the other hand, that time-place matrix of Antipas' intention and Tiberias' foundation in 20 CE, answers the questions that opened this chapter. *It also explains why, as Antipas moved from inland Sepphoris to lakeside Tiberias, Jesus counter-moved from inland Nazareth to lakeside Capernaum:* "He left Nazareth and made his home in Capernaum by the sea" (Matthew 4:13). By doing so, Jesus made a decisive decision to go where the action was brewing and where the suffering was most acute.

Think of what Herod Antipas' "enclosure" did to small peasant-fishers for whom the lake had once been an aquatic "commons" available to all who could afford a hook, a net, or, even if corporately, a boat. If they could still do any of that, Herod Antipas' monopoly meant enforced sale at fixed prices to his fish depots. By exploiting the farmers and peasants inland, Antipas had learned to multiply loaves in the land around Sepphoris; and by exploiting the fishermen and surrounding fishing villages, he would now learn how to multiply fishes in the lake around Tiberias. For small local fishers by the 20s, the once-open Lake of Galilee was the now-closed Lake of Tiberias.

Prior to change in moving the capitol and the renaming of the Sea of Galilee, these open waters provided sustenance and a way of life for many first-century Mediterranean families. The privatization and commercialization of the Sea of Galilee, which became Lake Tiberius, generated tremendous profit for Herod Antipas and the Roman Empire.

Conversely, the lake's rapid commercialization produced immense suffering and economic and physical strain for the families and fishing communities that lived and worked along those shores. Jesus, as organizers and activists often do, understood that if you are seeking to build a movement, you need to ask the question "Who are my people?" and "What are their primary concerns, fears and challenges?" In order to identify a community of people who are willing to join a cause for justice and righteousness, you must go to where the struggle and *action* is most dramatic.

Making the decision to go to where the action bristles is something that Ella Baker, Mahatma Gandhi, Martin Luther King, Dolores Huerta and other faith-rooted organizers also courageously demonstrated during their public lives. In the early 1960's, Martin Luther King Jr. and the Southern Christian Leadership Conference (SCLC) made the risky decision to organize a desegregation campaign in Birmingham, Alabama. At that time, Birmingham was also known as "Bombingham" because of the frequency of bombings that targeted African American activist organizers and were carried out by the Ku Klux Klan (KKK). Birmingham was also known for its rampant culture of police brutality under Commissioner of Public Safety Eugene "Bull" Conner. Birmingham was known as a place to be avoided. And, yet, it is where King and other SCLC leaders staged one of their most publicly dramatic and successful campaigns. They went where the struggle and *action* was.

Another example of this can be highlighted through the story of Dolores Huerta and the broader farmworker movement in California. Huerta spent decades working alongside communities of farm workers and day laborers whose lives were shaped by brutally long hours, poverty wages, and limited legal protections. Rather than turn away from the harsh conditions that defined migrant labor camps and rural fields, Huerta and the UFW chose to confront the systemic inequalities and power imbalances between the haves and have-nots. She and the UFW dedicated themselves to organizing farmworkers who lived in unforgiving places and worked in inhumane conditions. Again, she went to where the real struggle and action was, as Jesus did.

In direct response to the ruthless commercialization of the Sea of Galilee, Jesus went to where the action was. This was a profoundly risky choice. His decision to go where Herod Antipas was investing tremendous resources to exploit the local fishing villagers directly exposed him to the wide array of Roman collaborators and local military forces that were invested in Antipas' booming lakefront enterprise. This decision also reveals Jesus' clarity about who he wanted to invite into his growing Reign of God movement. The crisis of exploitation for the villagers along Lake Tiberias presented an opportunity for these communities to absorb the deeper spiritual and theological implications of Jesus' message. Within this context, Jesus' parables about calming turbulent waters (Matthew 8:23-26) and feeding masses of hungry people (Matthew 14:13-21) with the little remaining fish that was not shipped off to be sold, but left for them to share, were packed with explosive theological, political and economic significance.

The profound social, political and economic upheavals that Jesus' people were enduring along coastal villages of Lake Tiberias made it such that these parables would have been immediately understood as directly responding to the chaos, suffering and pain that Herod Antipas' ruthless commercialization of the lake and region was causing. The onslaught of economic exploitation and the various ways that they were squeezed financially, physically and emotionally made daily life a brutal reality. Rampant hunger and poverty made the political and economic instability and turbulence all the more painful and frightening.

Jesus' parables spoke to these realities. They offered comfort to those who toiled and suffered daily on the lake and along the shores. They also directly challenged the unholy alliance of powerful forces and the ideological underpinnings that produced and justified such suffering. Jesus' Reign of God offered a profound alternative to Rome's imperial vision and Herod Antipas' commercialization program. Within the Reign of God as one would find abundance, compassion, care and egalitarianism in contrast to the Roman Empire's foundation built upon an order of scarcity and domination.

Jesus' teaching through parables and his embodying of the unfolding vision and reality of God's Reign on Earth through his encounters, miracles, and by breaking bread demonstrated a communally collaborative and participatory approach throughout his public ministry. This approach was distinct in important ways from the vision and practice of John the Baptist as we will explore in the next section.

THE VISION OF THE HISTORICAL BAPTIST

In 597-587 BCE, the Babylonians conquered the Jews and took Jerusalem's elite leadership into so-called "Babylonian Exile" or "Babylonian Captivity." Then, in 538 BCE, the Babylonian Empire fell to the Persian Empire whose foreign policy was to restore conquered peoples so that they could pay imperial taxation. In that ecstatic moment, a Jewish prophet proclaimed that the Persian emperor, Cyrus the Great, was God's Messiah (Isaiah 45:1). Furthermore, in a rhapsodic image, that same prophet announced this divine command (Isaiah 40:3):

A voice cries out:

| "In the wilderness | prepare | the way | of the Lord, |
| In the desert | make straight | a highway | for our God" |

A heavenly voice commanded the desert/wilderness to prepare a direct and easy route by which God would lead the exiles home from Babylon to Jerusalem.

Compare, for a moment, the much earlier Exodus from Egypt with the much later Return from Exile. Both involved: a liberation from imperial domination, a passage across the desert, a transit of the Jordan river, and a climactic entrance into the Promised Land. But the Exodus was slow and hard, difficult and dangerous, across the desert northward from Egypt. The Return, by contrast, and at least in the idyll of Isaiah, would be swift and smooth along a divinely commanded highway homeward. Idealistic hyperbole, certainly, and more from Babylon before the Return started than from Jerusalem after it ended there.

Still, be that it may, Mark 1:3 applied that text from Isaiah 40:3 to John the Baptist, but parsed it out like this (in literal Greek translation):

The voice of one crying out in the wilderness:

| "Prepare | the way | of the Lord, |
| Make straight | the paths | of him" |

In other words, it is now the *voice* that is in the wilderness rather than *way/paths* that are there. That change is emphasized by the next sentence: "John the baptizer appeared in the wilderness proclaiming..." so that the voice is now from John on earth rather than from God in heaven. (It is therefore from Mark 1:3's rereading of Isaiah 40:3 that we get the cliché about "a voice crying in the wilderness" for a warning accurate but unheeded.) But, after all of that, what is at stake in that change from *God crying out—to prepare in the wilderness* (Isaiah) and *John crying out in the wilderness—to prepare* (Mark)? The answer needs three steps.

First, about half a millennium after Isaiah's ecstatic dream of returning from Babylonian imperial exile outside their homeland, Jews were now under Roman imperial "exile" inside it. Why, they must have asked John, does God allow this present oppression? His answer was the traditional prophetic one derived from Deuteronomy 28 that their sin involved divine punishment, garbed now in a toga.

Next, John had a very helpful and hopeful solution for their sinful situation. We will symbolically reenact the ancient salvific Return from Exile. We will go into the eastern desert-wilderness and cross thence through the Jordan back into the Promised Land. Then, as a newly-purified people, God would surely intervene as before and Roman power would disappear. All the endured oppression would end. But was that all a magical rite or a superstitious ritual? If not, why and how?

Finally, in answer, we can understand why Mark mentions that John "appeared in the wilderness, proclaiming a baptism of repentance for the forgiveness of sins" and that "people ... were baptized by him in the river Jordan, confessing their sins" (1:4-5). As they passed through the Jordan, water would wash their bodies as repentance would wash their souls, and only then would they re-enter the land as a purified people.

John gave people something to do that was actively communal, something that was at once completely novel but also mysteriously traditional, something beyond simply praying, hoping, and waiting for God to act. It still presumed that divine intervention was the solution to imperial oppression but, at least, with John, they could do something to prepare for or maybe even hasten its advent. John's vision was powerful, popular, and persuasive.

Josephus also knew John's nickname as the Baptist but he says nothing about any exilic reenactment or any transit from the desert through the Jordan into the land. All of that was probably too biblically Jewish for Greco-Roman readers. Instead, having completely omitted John's recapitulation of the Return from Exile, he defends from superstition a baptismal ritual he never clearly explains. John, he says, "had exhorted the Jews to lead righteous lives ... and so doing to join in baptism ... [as] a necessary preliminary if baptism was to be acceptable to God" (*Jewish Antiquities* 18.117).

Come back, one last time, to that change in the parsing of Isaiah 40:3 in Mark 1:3 and its shift from the voice of God *about* the desert-wilderness to that of John in it. Like John the Baptist—and like Jesus of Nazareth—we must learn to distinguish between their presence in history and their portrayal in the gospel, between what can be reconstructed historically and what is conveyed through evangelical interpretation.

On the one hand, the *historical* John prepared the way for the coming of God with his Exilic recapitulation and his Jordan-Baptism movement. (It had, of course, to be *in the Jordan* and not, say, in the Sea of Galilee.) On the other hand, the *evangelical* John prepared the way for the coming of Jesus and, thus, in our canonical presentation, the preparation for Jesus in Mark 1:1-8 leads immediately to the presentation of Jesus in 1:9-11.

Unfortunately, what came for John was not God's deliverance, in Gospel, but Antipas' cavalry, in both Gospel and Josephus (*JA* 118-119). John died, executed by Antipas in his fortress-palace at Machaerus in southern Perea—as far away from Galilee as was possible within his own territory. John died, and God did not come. John died, and God did nothing to prevent it. What was wrong—the timing or maybe the theology of God's advent?

The theological vision of God's imminent intervention proclaimed by John the Baptist was quite appealing, in part, because John's audience desperately wanted their present suffering to swiftly end. Not only were they eager for it to end, they were also eager for those who were responsible (Rome and its local collaborators) to be punished. Jesus certainly understood the persuasiveness and appeal of John's theology and movement, so much so that he himself was baptized by John.

Amidst the crushing poverty and constant threat of violence that was commonplace for Rome's colonized and conquered populations, it is certainly understandable that a desperate and yearning desire to escape from their present reality was common amongst first-century Jews during this time. Throughout history, many other groups of oppressed, colonized and enslaved people have very similarly found temporary solace in awaiting God's imminent intervention and divine judgment. Theologies that encourage passive awaiting often emerge and take root in religious contexts when hopelessness sets in and when it is commonly believed there is no possibility of changing the conditions that produce suffering. This experience is all the more acute when people feel rendered entirely powerless in the face of overwhelming power such as was the case for Jesus and his people under Roman occupation.

Throughout his public ministry, Martin Luther King Jr. spoke of the dangers of passivity and apathy in light of the persistent evils of racism, poverty and militarism. King's persistent warning about one's life "begins to end the moment you start being silent about things that matter" is as timely today as it was during his lifetime.

Passively awaiting God's eventual intervention is a failure to recognize the presence of God and the Holy Spirit in our lives and in the courageous acts of hope and resilience carried out by faithful Christians. Furthermore, it is an abdication of our agency and gifts when we do not organize collective grassroots power to effectively curb and challenge systems of oppression and foster a more just, humane and equitable society.

Today, this type of theological conviction surfaces when Christians proclaim Jesus' second coming as a justification for their own apathy and hopelessness. This theological outlook, combined with a resignation about political and economic affairs, also leads people to abdicate their agency and civil liberties to autocratic figures. Over the course of the 2024 presidential election season, Donald Trump urged conservative Christians to vote for him in part, because it meant that he would solve all their problems and they would never need to vote again.

While John the Baptist spoke out verbally against the evils of the Roman Empire and the personal transgressions of Herod Antipas, his movement did not exert organized grassroots pressure against Rome's system of domination and relentless exploitation. John the Baptist issued verbal castigations and criticisms against Rome and Herod Antipas, but he did not encourage his followers to seek to nonviolently confront Roman power and domination. John was eventually imprisoned and summarily executed by Herod Antipas. While John's vision and message foretold God's impending judgment and intervention, neither ever came. *The end times did not arrive.* Herod Antipas was not divinely punished. The wheels of Rome's oppression and domination did not halt or slow down. Business continued as usual for Herod Antipas and Rome's local collaborators following John's brutal execution and death.

THE CONVERSION OF JESUS THE NAZARENE

That Jesus began his public career at the Jordan by accepting John's theological vision, following his symbolic ritual, and participating in his communal reentrance is as assured as historical reconstruction can ever be—for two reasons.

One reason is the diffidence or even embarrassment with which the gospel writers record Jesus' baptism by John:

Mark simply admits it (1:9)
Matthew noisily argues it (3:13-15)
Luke barely hints it (3:21a)
John completely omits it (replaced by 1:29-34)

Another reason is that Jesus' subjection to John by baptism is immediately swallowed up by God's voice declaring Jesus to be God's son; the water from John is very deliberately overshadowed by the dove from God (Mark 1:10-11; Matthew 3:16-17; Luke 3:21b-22; John 1:32-34).

For those reasons, it is best to begin the not-yet-very-public life of the historical Jesus as one among the crowds accepting John's visionary ritual. But what happened to Jesus' commitment when Antipas came and God did not, when John died in lonely isolation, and when God did nothing to prevent that fate? Was it all a minor mistake in John's timing or a major one in John's theology?

Jesus could have simply picked up the fallen banner of John and continued his baptismal ritual from desert through Jordan to the (re) promised land. There was even a perfect biblical precedent for that solution: Elisha had taken up the mantle of the departed Elijah, crossed over the Jordan from east to west, and himself fulfilled Elijah's divine assignment (1 Kings 19:15-16; 2 Kings 2:13-14).

That, however, was not what happened. Jesus' solution was not a simple retiming of God's imminent advent but a profound conversion about God's intention. John's vision was of God's *future-imminent* salvific *intervention*, an intrusion by divinity into humanity. Jesus' conversion from John's vision was of God's *present-already* salvific *collaboration* between divinity and humanity. ("Covenant," of course, had always meant cooperation and collaboration.) What is the evidence for that conversion?

First, even contemporary opponents of both John and Jesus recognized there was something rather different between their two messages. Leaving aside any name-calling, here is the core of that divergence: "John came neither eating nor drinking" but then Jesus "came eating and drinking" (Matthew 11:18-19 = Luke 7:33-34). That speaks, in other words, of *fasting versus feasting*. But fasting is in preparation for what is coming soon (like Lent before Easter) while feasting is in celebration for what has already come (like Easter after Lent).

Next, Jesus treats John like a revered mentor whom he will not criticize but with whom he no longer agrees: "I tell you, among those born of women no one has arisen greater than John the Baptist; yet the least in the kingdom of God is greater than he" (Matthew 11:11 = Luke 7:28).

Furthermore, Jesus proclaims that the Reign of God, that is, God on Earth, is already present and already evident in his own power to deliver from demonic possession: "if it is by the Spirit [*or* Finger] of God that I cast out demons, then the kingdom of God has come to you" (Matthew 12:28 = Luke 11:20).

Finally, is—and how is—the medium of Jesus' teaching especially appropriate to Jesus' message of God's rule as already (and always?) present—as a participatory divine challenge pending human cooperation and collaboration?

Jesus' parables are probably his most strikingly memorable mode of teaching ("Good Samaritan" and "Prodigal Son" are permanent clichés.) But what is the connection between Jesus' teaching as parabolic and Jesus' message of God's Reign as present? Parables challenge the hearer's participation by interpretation and application: we know it's not about sowing, so what is it about? *Parables are the participatory pedagogy of Jesus for a participatory Reign of God.*

The profound message that Jesus conveyed to his hearers through participatory parables and participatory actions ("feeding of many with fish and loaves" and "encounter with the woman at the well") was that their active *collaboration* and *participation* was required for God's Reign to become manifest on earth. Jesus' spiritual genius recognized the need for the oppressed ("fishermen" and "women"), marginalized ("woman at the well" and "Bartimaeus") and converted ("tax collectors") to be engaged protagonists in God's *participatory* revolution on earth. It is this brilliant insight - that the people who are closest to the problem are central to the solution - that community organizing, at its best, seeks to advance across the public sphere.

The notion that God's Reign was springing forth in their midst was a startling claim, most especially because of the very visible and dominating presence of the Roman Empire in their everyday lives. This would have been a stunning message for Jesus' listeners and followers to believe and embrace. A key reason for this is that systems of oppression and domination not only produce harsh political, economic and social material conditions, they also wage war on the spiritual, emotional and psychological psyches of communities and their sense of worthiness and inner confidence.

Part of the dehumanizing and disempowering process which empires and autocracies carry out involves convincing people that they in fact are the ones, and not the powerful and wealthy, who are responsible for their own impoverishment and suffering. This creates the illusion of false dependency where imperial rulers and autocrats claim they are the ones who will provide stability, security and prosperity. They will solve society's problems. They will save the world. This was true within the Roman Empire (Augustus "Prince of Peace" and "Savior of the World") and this pattern persists 2,000 years later as many self-proclaimed Christians and Christian organizations have characterized Donald Trump as being divinely chosen by God to "save" the United States.

Overcoming such depths of self-doubt, hopelessness and timidness within his own people, and transforming it into a collective sense of hope, spiritual conviction and engaged protagonism is one of the oft unspoken miracles of Jesus' nonviolent Reign of God movement. Although 2,000 years have passed since Jesus challenged the reign of the Roman Empire, human affairs continue to be dictated by a small number of remarkably powerful political elites and corporate titans. One of the primary tasks that we are called to participate in today is continuing to follow and embody Jesus' *theology of collaboration*.

The beloved Anglican Archbishop from South Africa, Desmond Tutu, beautifully paraphrased St. Augustine's famous saying, capturing the essence of the interdependent relationship between God and humanity, when he often repeated: "God, without us, will not; as we, without God, cannot." Tutu's words were a source of inspiration and encouragement to the many

Christian organizers and activists in South Africa who were engaged in the anti-apartheid struggle to build a free and democratic nation. They also reflect the theological and spiritual genius of Jesus' *theology of collaboration*. Today, faith-rooted community organizing, student activism, labor strikes, anti-war campaigns and other grassroots civic efforts are examples of ways in which God's people are striving to change society through a bottom-up process of *participatory* engagement and divine *collaboration*.

Perhaps nothing more definitively captures the revolutionary spirit of Jesus' Reign of God movement and its continuation in our world today than God's conviction that each of us, and most especially those who are poor and dispossessed, *should, can, and must* have a decisive say in the political, economic and social decisions which affect our lives. There is a beautiful saying in community organizing that goes "nothing about us, without us, is for us." This organizing proverb speaks to the transformative power of bottom-up grassroots organizing. Just as modern grassroots organizing coalitions and social movements rely on the engaged participation of everyday people, the history of Jesus' world is also rooted in the lives and labor of ordinary individuals. One remarkable discovery from that time— the Ancient Galilee Boat—offers a tangible connection to those everyday people and the world they lived in.

THE ANCIENT GALILEE BOAT

In 1985-1986, an extreme drought lowered the level of the Sea of Galilee and exposed the lakebed near ancient Tarichaeae, about six miles north of Tiberias. In late January of 1986, Moshe and Yuval Lufan, brothers, fishers, and amateur archeologists from Kibbutz Ginosar, to the nearby north of Tarichaeae, discovered a 27-foot boat from the first-century CE buried in that stretch of bared lake-bottom.

With the lake waters rising, an immediate salvage excavation was necessary. First, the waterlogged boat was completely enveloped with hardened polyurethane foam that hardened into a protective cocoon. Then, the ensemble was floated to a preservation tank newly constructed for it at the Yigal Allon Centre in Kibbutz Ginosar. Next, over a 14-year period, polyethylene glycol (PEG) slowly replaced the water that had reduced the boat's consistency to that of wet cardboard. Finally, the magnificently

preserved boat was put on public display in a special room at the Centre dedicated to "The Ancient Galilee Boat."

This is certainly the *type* of workhorse boat used for fishing and transporting cargo or clients in the lake's first century CE. It is also the boat *imagined* for Jesus and his companions in the gospels. But that is not why we mention it here. It is, of course, only one example of that boat-*type* but also the only such first-century boat ever found in fresh water. Still, we emphatically do not use that boat as proof, argument, or evidence for anything but as an emblem, symbol, or even sacrament for everything. *We take it as an icon of the clash between Antipas' Reign of Rome and Jesus' Reign of God as the Sea of Galilee was transformed into the Sea of Tiberias in the 20s CE.*

This oared sailing boat, built in a boatyard at its findspot, was initially constructed and regularly repaired by more-than-adequate boatwrights working with less-than-adequate materials. The original keel, for example, joined together both suitable cedar-wood from Lebanon—but taken from some abandoned boat—and rather unsuitable local jujube (also known as Christ Torn wood, traditionally linked to the crown of thorns). Worn from years of use and cobbled together by 12 different types of wood, it was finally no longer sailable, was stripped of everything still usable for repairing other boats, pushed out into the lake, and allowed to sink into the mud and rest there for two thousand years.

The two nautical archeologists who first excavated the Galilee Boat discussed its somewhat desperate lifespan in Shelley Wachsmann's 1995 book, *The Sea of Galilee Boat: An Extraordinary 2000 Year Old Discovery* (New York: Plenum Press).

John Richard Steff, a visiting American expert, commented that, "The Kinneret boat seemed to be made up entirely of a crazy-quilt patchwork construction ... The boatwright who put this boat together knew exactly what he was doing ... but he was using inferior materials ... using recycled timber ... There is something pathetic about this hull" (pp. 142, 143,147).

Shelley Wachsmann, the resident Jewish expert noted that, "The Galilee at this time was economically depressed ... the timbers used in the boat's construction are perhaps a physical expression of this overall economic situation" (p. 358).

There is, however, no evidence for a generally depressed economic situation in Antipas' Galilean 20s and, if there were, he might not have lasted the next twenty years as its ruler. Indeed, Antipas' commercialization and monetization, monopoly and control of the lake's fishing was probably the engine of a boom in his economy. The question, however, is not whether Antipas' economy boomed but *for whom did it boom, for whom did it not boom, and for whom did it change things so much worse than they were before.*

What does this dingy and pathetic first-century Galilean fishing boat have to teach us about Jesus' concern with the commercialization of the Sea of Galilee? What, if any, connection connection can we draw between this boat and the economic pressures that people face today? If you were to drive through lower-income neighborhoods, farmlands and small working-class towns today you may periodically or perhaps quite often see a pickup truck pieced and parceled together from various parts. Just as the excavated first-century Galilean boat was made up of patchwork construction, there are countless trucks that are similarly kept together through patchwork construction and have the appearance of a multi-colored quilt.

Upon visiting your big-box hardware and construction store you are bound to see trucks with all sorts of parts that have been bolted, welded or taped on them. These car parts rarely match the original color of the truck. You might find a black truck with a red bumper on the front and a blue bumper on the back. A green door on one side of the truck and the original black door on the other side, albeit heavily dented and discolored. The parts on these trucks are often hanging on with bungee cords or rope. A broken window is covered in tape or plastic. Each of the four tires represent a different brand and size. One can only imagine how many parts from various other trucks have been transplanted from one engine to another.

The image of a truck with a diverse assortment of parts that have been taped, bolted and welded on is a contemporary reflection of the sunken boat from first-century Galilee. The owners of these trucks are often economically pinched and under constant pressure to find their next job. As Michael's father did, these workers petition God each day for a miracle - that their truck will start when they begin their long day of work before the sun has risen.

Today, as was the case during Jesus' lifetime, these workers earn meager wages, receive no healthcare and live precariously day to day. Just as this boat is a symbol of the economic squeeze that families endured along Lake Tiberias, the patch-quilt trucks that drive through our cities, towns and villages daily represent that economic squeeze that millions of families endure in our world today.

Jesus traveled to where the suffering and struggles for Galileans was most dramatic. He was drawn to Lake Tiberias precisely because it is where Herod Antipas' political and economic activity was roaring. It was along these shores where Jesus encountered many of the disciples that were invited and drawn into his nonviolent movement. Simon, Andrew, James and John were all fishermen who lived, worked, and toiled during the commercialization of the Sea of Galilee.

One could imagine then why they were deeply drawn to Jesus' message of God's Reign. While Herod Antipas' economy of *scarcity, intimidation,* and *extraction* was in full swing, Jesus' movement spoke through the use of pedagogical and participatory parables and deeds that made manifest God's *abundance* in the face of scarcity, God's *love* in the midst of fear, and God's *justice* when injustice was so pervasive.

Many other social movements and leaders have rooted their ministry and work in communities where misery, suffering, and injustice were pervasive. Ella Baker, the remarkable civil rights organizer who co-founded the Student Nonviolent Coordinating Committee (SNCC), served as a director with the NAACP and was the first staff member hired as Associate Director to run the Southern Christian Leadership Conference, traveled all over southern cities and towns during the Jim Crow era.

She traveled extensively throughout Georgia, Alabama, Mississippi and other southern states during a period when the KKK, white citizens councils, and local law enforcement agencies ruthlessly terrorized and brutalized African-American communities with impunity. There she worked to organize and launch voter registration drives and campaigns to address local social, political, and economic grievances. She traveled to southern cities and towns where most organizers and activists were too intimidated and afraid to go, because organizing any form of grassroots resistance in these places came at great risk.

Many organizers, activists and people of faith today build and foster meaningful relationships with local grassroots leaders and communities in neighborhoods, towns, and villages that few desire to visit. As Jesus modeled over two thousand years ago through his encounters and conversations with his apostles and followers, organizers today travel to places where injustice is far too common. In their encounters with people, they listen intently to their stories and struggles. They respond with understanding and compassion.

Most significantly, they invite them into the important and holy enterprise of organizing, where with others they break bread, build relationships, foster community, strategize, discern, pray, and take action - all of which leads to meaningful change in their lives. These are the people, both local grassroots leaders and organizers, whom Pope Francis referred to as today's "social poets" because they seek to foster justice and peace wherever they go.

TRADITION AND TRACTION

Antipas' plan for the Galilean 20s involved the construction of lakeside Tiberias as his new capital; the commercialization of the lake from that power-base; the monopolistic control of fishing by and for his fish-factories; and, finally the monetization of the lake's fishes for export—from the Sea *of Tiberias*. Think now what that did to local peasants who, before all of that, had freely and openly used the lake for shore-based or even boat-based fishing with cast or seine-net—in the Sea *of Galilee*.

There is even a name for what happened to those locals: they lost *piscary* rights. Even if fishing rights were still permitted, they were probably taxed and/or their products acquired at fixed prices by Antipas' fish factories. Across history, that is how areas open to the many become areas open only to the few, how *commons* once open to the "have-nots" become *enclosures* open only to the "haves".

In the 700s BCE, Isaiah had deplored, "you who join house to house, who add field to field, until there is room for no one but you, and you are left to live alone in the midst of the land!" (5:8). In the 20s CE, Jesus agreed: "To those who have, more will be given; and from those who have nothing, even what they have will be taken away" (Mark 4:25 = Matthew 13:12 = Luke 8:18). That applies to the greed-grasp not just for land and houses or lake and fishes but for anything that one person may have and another may desire.

In the 20s, Antipas had relocated his base from inland Sepphoris to lakeside Tiberias. At that same time, and on almost a parallel track, Jesus had relocated his base from inland Nazareth to lakeside Capernaum. Jesus' vision was the tradition of Torah, Prophecy, and Wisdom that the produce of the world should be distributed fairly among all its people (Genesis 1). Jesus' tradition was not new, but his time and place were, and that time and place gave traction to tradition. It meant, for example, that small-time fishers or local observers were not just hearing about God's ideal of distributive justice but feeling its absence practically and viscerally. So:

> As Jesus passed along the Sea of Galilee, he saw Simon and his brother Andrew casting a net into the sea—for they were fishermen. And Jesus said to them, "Follow me and I will make you fish for people." And immediately they left their nets and followed him. As he went a little farther, he saw James, son of Zebedee, and his brother John, who were in their boat mending the nets. Immediately he called them; and they left their father Zebedee in the boat with the hired men, and followed him. (Mark 1:16-20)

Tradition without traction is lame; traction without tradition is blind. And the first eucharist in Mark was not bread and wine but bread and fish—that too was traction. Tradition announced: "the earth is the Lord's and all that is in it" (Psalm 24:1). Traction inquired: then whose is the lake and all of its fishes?

In a contemporary sense, the coalescing of tradition and traction contributed to the significant emergence of important social movements at various times throughout the 20th and 21st centuries. The Solidarity movement in Poland, the Civil Rights movement in the U.S., the Anti-Apartheid struggle in South Africa and the Indian independence movement are all examples where within these movements both elements of tradition and traction were mutually present and reinforced. In each of these examples, religious and cultural traditions were powerful and inspiring forces that served to ground, galvanize, and sustain these movements.

Today, it is vitally important that we reinvigorate the very best of what our religious traditions offer. Jesus was deeply rooted in the Jewish prophetic tradition. Christian and Catholic communities have immense spiritual and theological resources to draw upon. What is essential in this process is that we draw upon the parts of our traditions that maintain continuity and connection to the prophetic roots that deeply inspired and informed Jesus' vision and public ministry. Understanding traction comes through a process of discerning the signs of the times and going to where the suffering is most acute and profound. Whether that is along our borders, neighborhoods with high levels of violence, villages and towns that have experienced profound disinvestment or communities where global warming has created profound environmental instability and uncertainty, going to these places and listening to the people who are closest to the problems invokes the spirit and example of Jesus.

CHAPTER 2

THE EXECUTION OF JESUS

The preceding chapter focused on John and Jesus in Galilee under Herod Antipas. John was executed and that probably saved Jesus for another day and another place. Antipas, "that fox" (Luke 13:32), knew better than to execute a second popular prophet too soon after the first one. Doing so would have risked triggering an uprising, which he was eager to avoid. This chapter, however, is no longer about Jesus and the Jewish client-prince Herod Antipas in Galilee, but about Jesus and the Roman prefect-governor Pontius Pilate, in Jerusalem, at Passover, in 30 CE.

Also, as you expect after the preceding chapter, our historical method *starts* with the critical reading not only of texts within the New Testament, like Mark and John, but also of contemporary ones from outside it, like Josephus and Tacitus. Still, if we start with history then, we end with history now, and always. Then and now, there is the challenge of theology as the meaning of history.

PASSOVER, PILATE AND CRUCIFIXION

What do we know about the situation at Jerusalem during Passover before and after Jesus' demonstrations there in 30 CE? In the Apostles Creed, Pontius Pilate appears without explanation of who or what he was. What do we know about the political function and character of Pilate? Above all else, what do we know about crucifixion as state terrorism in Judea and Galilee under Romanization?

The Dangers of Passover

Imagine the situation: the Temple complex was five football fields from north to south and three from east to west. Huge crowds filled those courts for the sacrifice of the paschal lambs which were then eaten at home. *They were celebrating divine deliverance from past Egyptian imperial bondage while under present Roman imperial bondage.* That the Passover celebration of the Exodus was held in the Temple within the context of Roman imperial domination, made this religious ritual and event politically charged. To be reminded of that situation, they only had to look up from their sacrifices to the soldiers on the ramparts of the Antonia Fortress overlooking the Temple at its northwest corner.

This point must be underscored - revolutionary stories and memories inspire revolutions. In the case of the ritual of Passover, the political and religious dynamics inherent in this audacious narrative of liberation are inseparable from one another. The celebration of their freedom from Egyptian bondage, while under Roman bondage and surrounded by Roman soldiers, carried profound political and religious implications. Was this arrangement an affront to God's will? How could one reconcile celebrating a story of freedom while suffering under the yoke of imperial domination? What would happen if somebody shouted dissent, invoked remembrance, or incited resistance?

Furthermore, if dissent became riot and those soldiers streamed down into the Temple courts, many more people would be killed in a crushing rush for the southern exits than by the punitive onslaught of the soldiers themselves. Here, for example, are two such Passover riots, one before and one after Jesus' Passover of 30 CE.

In 4 BCE, in reaction to Herod the Great's order of execution against popular activist teachers, Josephus reported that:

At the Feast of ... Passover ... it did not appear ... that the multitude could be restrained without bloodshed; so he [Archelaus] sent his whole army ... who, falling upon them on the sudden, as they were offering their sacrifices, destroyed about three thousand of them." (*Jewish War* 2:10-13 = Jewish Antiquities 17. 213-218)[1]

As you recall from our last chapter, Augustus had appointed Archelaus as ruler of Judea on the death of his father, Herod the Great. When Jesus was asked "about the Galileans whose blood Pilate had mingled with their sacrifices," that may be a mistaken allusion to that earlier Passover riot (Luke 13:1).

Be that as it may, there was an even more serious Passover riot in 50 CE under Cumanus as the Roman governor of all Judea:

At Passover ... a great multitude was gathered together .... but on the fourth day of the feast, a certain soldier let down his breeches, and exposed his privy members to the multitude, which put those that saw him into a furious rage ... Cumanus [sent his] whole army ... [from the] Antonia, which was a fortress ... which overlooked the temple ... and a great number were pressed to death in those narrow passages; no fewer than twenty thousand perished in this tumult. (*JA* 20.106-112 = *JW* 2.224-227, but with "ten thousand" dead)

Those examples make it clear why Pilate brought extra military troops from his base at coastal Caesarea to enforce the Antonia for Passover and would have had them quartered there in 30 CE. If, however, Passover was a volatile situation, Pilate was a savage principal figure.

History is replete with examples of political and military authorities who have ruthlessly deployed armed forces to suppress and crack down on grassroots uprisings and social movements. Anti-apartheid organizers and leaders in South Africa faced persistent risk of death, imprisonment and

---

[1] The complete works of Josephus are available fully and freely online in the Christian Classics Ethereal Library. In case you are interested in reading the evidence for yourself, we will always give you the references from Josephus using the abbreviations *JW* for *Jewish War* (70s CE) and *JA* for *Jewish Antiquities* (90s CE).

torture at the hands of the South African Police (SAP). At the behest of the apartheid government, the SAP ruthlessly quelled protests and marches by means of brutal and violent measures throughout the entire anti-apartheid movement.

The Sharpeville Massacre in 1960 is a painfully vivid example of this. According to police records, at least 69 anti-apartheid protesters were shot and killed and another 180 were injured at a protest outside a police station when SAP officers opened fire on protestors. However, more recent research suggests that at least 91 people were killed and at least 238 were wounded. Many of the protestors who were killed and wounded that day, including women and children, were shot in the back as they desperately fled the firing officers.

Saint Oscar Romero's public assassination during a Mass he was celebrating is another example of a brutal government deploying military forces to suppress a growing social and religious liberation movement. As the Romans understood and practiced, grassroots social movements could be severely diminished when their high-profile leaders were killed. The U.S.-trained military death squad that was responsible for the assassination of Archbishop Oscar Romero in March of 1980 was also responsible for countless atrocities against poor campesinos (peasants) and grassroots leaders. Thousands of poor Salvadoran Catholics who were involved through their church and local community groups in efforts to organize for their economic and human rights were kidnapped, killed, and tortured by Salvadoran government backed and U.S.-trained military death squads.

In their cruel determination to quell the growing uprising of workers and campesinos and to prevent Archbishop Romero from becoming a martyr whose death would further inspire Catholic campesinos, the governmental and military forces in El Salvador carried out a massacre during Archbishop Romero's funeral held at the San Salvador Cathedral. Gunshots rang out from surrounding buildings, including from inside the National Palace. The powerful alignment of political, military, and economic authorities in El Salvador labeled Archbishop Romero and the many Catholic parishioners and groups "communists" in order to undermine and delegitimize their rightful stance and protests against rampant human rights violations, economic exploitation and political repression.

The parallels between the violent and oppressive realities that Jesus' movement faced under Roman imperial domination are quite similar in many ways to the multitude of government-backed military and law enforcement campaigns that were carried in response to social movements in countries throughout the world during the 20th century. In the 21st century, movements and demonstrations for racial justice, land rights, immigrant rights, economic and environmental justice continue to be met with violent military and police force across the world.

The unholy alliance between powerful political, economic, military, and religious actors and institutions continues to be a pervasive reality in our contemporary world. It is a fateful combination that breeds conditions of profound misery for those it exploits. Social movements and grassroots organizations must always organize to nonviolently dismantle and transform the systems of death and exploitation that alliances between the ultra-rich and powerful produce. That is exactly what Jesus did with his Reign of God movement 2,000 years ago.

The politically explosive environment within and surrounding the Temple during Passover and the truly savage nature of the Roman Empire has been left out of the common accounts and broader Christian understanding of Holy Week. This fact gravely diminishes the profoundly courageous and truly militant (showing a bold forcefulness) character of Jesus' nonviolent demonstrations during that fateful last week of his life.

The Character of Pilate

Starting with Mark and intensifying in those three other gospel-versions using him as their basic sources, Pilate appears as a hypocritical weakling. He knows that Jesus is innocent, "for he realized that it was out of jealousy that the chief priests had handed him over" (15:10) and he challenged those accusers by asking, "'What evil has he done'"? (15:10, 14). Despite that awareness, when those "chief priests" stirred up the crowd ... Pilate wishing to satisfy the crowd ... after flogging Jesus, he handed him over to be crucified" (15:11,15).

On the one hand, as a governor submitting his judgment to a crowd "shouting" and then "shouting more" (15:13,14) for what they wanted, Pilate was portrayed by Mark as a caricature of Rome's vaunted legal justice. On the other hand, we know a lot about Pilate not only from Josephus but also from his older contemporary, Philo, the Jewish philosopher from Alexandra in Egypt. There, and there emphatically, Pilate is not portrayed as a weak judge but as a savage ruler.

Philo's description of Pilate is so unrelentingly terrible that you almost wonder could anyone be *that* bad. Still, Philo chose Pilate as a poster-boy for a bad Roman ruler, and we quote him here in full:

> [Pilate was] a man of very inflexible disposition, and very merciless as well as obstinate [because of] his corruption, and his acts of insolence, and his rapine, and his habit of insulting people, and his cruelty, and his continued murders of people untried and uncondemned, and his never ending, and gratuitous, and most grievous inhumanity .... being at all times a man of most ferocious passions ... briberies, insults, robberies, outrages, wanton injuries, constantly repeated executions without trial, ceaseless and supremely grievous cruelty. [*Embassy to Gaius-Caligula*, 302]

In any case, Pilate governed central and southern Judea from 26 to 36 CE but in that last year his immediate superior, Vitellius, the governor of Roman Syria, removed both him and the high-priest Caiaphas from office and ordered Pilate back to Rome to explain his actions (*JA* 18.89, 95). Both were, possibly in concert, too unpopular for even Rome to accept their cruelty. They were in fact *that* cruel and inhumane.

Pilate was hardly the first or the last authority figure to govern with an iron fist. Social movements and organizers have long had to contend with authorities who believed that cruelty was the most effective form of deterrence and suppression. In our previous chapter, we briefly discussed the terrible legacy of Birmingham's Safety Commissioner, Eugene Bull O'Conner. Another more contemporary example would be the former Arizona Sheriff of Maricopa County, Joe Apairo. Despite being the son of immigrants, his two-decade reign as sheriff exacted a terrible toll on immigrant communities across Arizona and garnered him celebrity status amongst xenophobic media outlets and organizations across the United States.

During his time as sheriff between 1993 and 2017, the jail population in Maricopa County exploded with undocumented immigrants who had never committed a crime. To save taxpayer money, Sheriff Apairo built a "tent city" in 1993 in the middle of the Arizona desert where temperatures would reach up to 118 degrees a day outside and up to 145 degrees within the tents - a decision that was made to push immigrants to their bodily limit. Arpaio referred to "tent city" as a "concentration camp" where he denied inmates their most basic necessities and cut the cost of their meals to 30 cents per day. He once bragged that it "costs more to feed the dogs."

He not only exacted physical cruelty on inmates but also waged psychological campaigns against those he incarcerated and also immigrant communities across Arizona by marching chained inmates together through the streets and deserts of Arizona. For years, organizers, immigrant rights organizations, faith-based organizations and civil rights attorneys challenged Sheriff Arpaio's cruel, scandalous and dehumanizing policies through protests, lawsuits and voter drives.

Sheriff Arpaio's brazen style of cruelty towards immigrants was once deemed an outlier in the U.S. law enforcement community, however, the explosion of xenophobic and anti-immigrant sentiment since his reign as sheriff ended in 2017 has become more politically mainstream and enthusiastically embraced. Cruelty and violence have often been deployed by agents of various states and empires to suppress movements and oppress entire populations. While there is a general understanding of this historical fact, broadly speaking, little attention has often been paid to Pontius Pilate's character and historical legacy, his role within the Roman Empire, and the environment of terror that he fostered. So much of that context is omitted from the Gospel texts.

Pilate's callous ease with ordering massacres at public events, points to the social context that defined Passover in first-century Jerusalem. The environment during this time was not to be confused with being volatile. Volatility can imply a degree of unpredictability and uncertainty. In quite the opposite manner, Pilate mercilessly fomented an atmosphere of cruel certitude.

Any step outside the line, however faintly or meekly, any public action or protest regardless of whether it was violent or nonviolent, carried the immediate sentence of persecution and swift punishment. This reality of unimaginable fear, cruelty and suffering was Jesus' reality. Despite the looming risk of death that hung over Jesus, he decided to carry out two profoundly risky and defiant demonstrations that were packed with the type of symbolism that was meant to stir and provoke a response.

The Terrorism of Crucifixion

In this case, the terrorism was not *against* the state but *by* the state. As a very particular Roman form of execution, crucifixion was not intended simply to prolong the pain nor intended to maximize the suffering and extend the torture of a victim. That preliminary flogging, for example, was intended to prevent any form of physical resistance all the way to the cross while ensuring the individual got there alive for crucifixion.

There was, of course attendant suffering, degradation, and dishonor—if the victim had any honor—but the primary purpose of Roman crucifixion was imperial terrorism: *if you act like that, you die like this!* But what terrorized you in that imperial spectacle was not the specter of personal suffering but the horror of individual eradication and social annihilation. *Because*: apart from bribing executioners or influencing authorities to allow burial, there would be nothing left to bury because wild dogs that roamed the lands would drag the victims corpses from the cross and consume them.

Think for example, of the compendium of Roman law by the famous Roman jurist, Julius Paulus Prudentissimus, from the 200s. In the section "Concerning Acquittals," he summarizes that, "Extreme punishments [*suprema supplicia*] are crucifixion, burning alive, beheading" (*The Opinions of Julius Paulus Addressed to His Son*, Book V, Title XVII, #3). Condemnation to feral beasts in the arena was also an extreme penalty, but such beasts and an arena safe for the audience from them was not always available. In all those cases, there was either nothing identifiable left for burial or it was simply not allowed and the best fate was the common death-pit, the worst fate the closest garbage-dump.

In that Roman world, when you saw a single person crucified as distinct from a multiple crucifixion, you would think of some sort of resistance to Romanization. But, even if it was that of a recalcitrant slave crucified by an individual master, it was also the perfect warning-symbol to an enslaved empire from an imperial master.

The only crucified skeleton found in Judea so far was from the first century, was named Yehohanan or John, was buried in an ossuary or bone-box, and was excavated in 1968 from an expensive tomb on the hilly suburb of Givat HaMivtar north of the Old City of Jerusalem. In best reconstruction: The crucified man had his almost-dislocated arms roped on top and behind the cross-beam while his ankles were attached one on either side of the upright by nails driven first through small olive-wood boards for added security. But the nail tip through the right ankle bent against a knot in the upright and remained in that heel bone for the next two thousand years. That is an individual example, not a universal model, because contempt and cruelty, savagery and sadism are always variables in such executions—then and now.

Why is this vivid description of the ruthless and deliberate practice of Roman crucifixion and Jesus' torture and execution relevant and important? For one, mainline Christianity and Catholicism has failed to nurture a collective sense of shock and horror at the truly barbarous nature of Jesus' violent death and the political campaign of terror that the Romans waged in response to Jesus' vision and nonviolent militancy. As a result, our understanding of Jesus' crucifixion is most often sentimentalized. We therefore lack an intellectually rigorous and clear-eyed political assessment of the Roman Empire's intention to scatter and destroy Jesus' nonviolent Reign of God movement.

Jesus' execution was planned and carried out by Pontius Pilate because Rome's imperial program of terrorizing, dominating, exploiting and co-opting its local subjects was directly and boldly challenged and denounced by Jesus and his nonviolent movement. The Roman Empire was certainly not the first, nor the last empire to deploy torture and capital punishment to terrorize and destroy grassroots movements.

Most commonly carried out in Southern territories across the United States, lynchings were systematically conducted by racist organizations, mobs and vigilantes, very often with complicit support and cooperation from U.S. law enforcement agencies and political authorities. Lynchings, similarly to Roman crucifixions, were performed in public view with the intended purpose of terrorizing African American communities.

African Americans who organized and advocated for their basic rights were targeted by white Southern terrorist groups of which the KKK was the most notorious. The explicit message that lynchings were intended to convey to African Americans was that any form of resistance to the white Southern racial, political and economic order *meant torture and execution.* In his work, *The Cross and the Lynching Tree*, James Cone the founder of Black Liberation Theology, spoke with forceful moral and historical clarity about the connection between Jesus' crucifixion within the Roman Empire and the African American experience with lynchings in the United States.

Just as Roman soldiers exercised brutal creativity in prolonging the torture of their victims before death and welcomed wild beasts to devour the body of their victims after death, an execution by lynching was rarely swift. Victims of lynchings were often shot, beat, dismembered, castrated, mutilated or burned alive before they were lynched. Their bodies were often left to burn as part of the barbaric spectacle and to ensure the complete annihilation of their victim's body.

Despite the 2,000 years that have passed since Jesus' crucifixion, many empires, governments, corporations, economic elites and extremist groups have developed and devised more contemporary ways of crucifying people who struggle and suffer daily. Jon Sobrino, the Spanish Jesuit priest who contributed to the development of Latin American Liberation Theology, coined the phrase "crucified people" to refer to the people in our world today who like Jesus are poor, marginalized and exploited and who suffer unjustly due to the tremendous imbalance of social, political and economic power.

Through the legal, political, technological and military means and methods that are available today, multinational corporations, political figures, and the ultra-wealthy continue to leverage their power to crucify those who resist injustice. Despite the terror and trauma of it all, Jesus' spirit of love and hope somehow persists in the lives of those who dream of and strive for justice.

DEMONSTRATIONS AS NONVIOLENT CHALLENGES

Why did Jesus go to Jerusalem? If Jesus went regularly, which is a doubtful financial option for what Mark calls a *tektōn* or day-laborer (6:3), what happened this one time? If Jesus only went this one time, why this time and what happened then? Did Jesus go to Jerusalem for deliberate martyrdom either as a vicarious atonement for sin in the later Protestant tradition or as an obedient model for suffering in the later Roman Catholic tradition? The following two parts present the answer, and they must be taken together. Both derive from interpreting Jesus' *actions* rather than reading Jesus' *mind*.

That Last Week in Mark

By general scholarly consensus, Mark is the major source for both Matthew and Luke. Also, although this is contested, for John as well. Therefore, to probe that first question about Jesus' purpose for that Passover in Jerusalem, we depend primarily on Mark. That is not, of course, as if Mark were straight history. It is rather openly and honestly "gospel" (Mark 1:1), that is, a theological interpretation of history as "good news." Still, among the gospels, it is *through* Mark that we can best reconstruct the general what, why, and wherefore of that fateful week, now known as Holy Week.

Look, in terms of *time*, at how Mark presents and emphasizes what we now call *Holy Week* as a day-by-day account of actions by, with, and to Jesus that Passover. Notice also, or especially, in terms of *place*, how day-by-day *time* correlates with daily transitions of *place*:

Sunday (11:1-11): "When they were approaching Jerusalem, at Bethphage and Bethany, near the Mount of Olives ... Then he entered Jerusalem and went into the temple; and when he had looked around at everything, as it was already late, he went out to Bethany with the twelve." Note the established sequence as: Bethany, Temple, Bethany.

Monday (11:12-19): "On the following day, when they came from Bethany ... they came to Jerusalem ... he entered the temple ... And when evening came, Jesus and his disciples went out of the city." Note the presumed sequence as Bethany, Temple, [Bethany].

Tuesday (11:20-13:37): "In the morning ... Again they came to Jerusalem ... he was walking in the temple." Note the presumed sequence as [Bethany], Temple, [Bethany].

Wednesday-Thursday (14:1-17): "It was two days before the Passover and the festival of Unleavened Bread... he was at Bethany in the house of Simon the leper ... 'Go into the city' ... went to the city ... When it was evening, he came with the twelve." Note the broken sequence as: Bethany, City, Arrest.

The Markan pattern of Jesus' actions is quite clear. Jesus does not stay overnight in Jerusalem. Instead, he stayed in Bethany which was the village of "Lazarus ... Mary and her sister Martha ... near Jerusalem, some two miles away" (John 11:1,18).

Question: Was Bethany for Jesus free lodging, family hospitality, or guaranteed safety? If Bethany was for night-time safety, what about day-time safety in Jerusalem and its Temple? Also, from whom was safety necessary? Once again, watch Mark's day-by-day account for those first four days but under that second rubric of day-time security.

The Protecting Crowd

Sunday (Mark 11:1-11). On what we call Palm Sunday, Jesus' entry into Jerusalem is described *as an already planned demonstration* (note Mark 11:2-6), as a calculated counter-entrance by donkey from eastward Bethany to Pilate's expected arrival by horse from westward Caesarea. (Notice that Matthew 21:4-5 sees here explicitly a fulfillment of Zechariah 9:9-10 as the Messiah enters Jerusalem in cosmic peace.) The reaction is that "many people" and "others" join enthusiastically in this demonstration against Pilate and Romanization, an action so dangerous in the tinder-box atmosphere and zero-toleration mood of *any* disturbance at Passover under Pilate.

Imagine the striking and bold public scene that Jesus' demonstration must have created during Passover in the midst of a sea of poor Jewish pilgrims who were gathered in Jerusalem for this holy occasion. Tensions between Roman authorities and the masses of gathered Jews would have been alarmingly high. Jesus' nonviolent procession of "many" poor peasants while riding a donkey was a public dramatization of the absurdity of the pomp and cruel spectacle of Pontius Pilate's imperial entrance while seated atop a war horse and surrounded by Roman soldiers adorned in their military garb. This nonviolent counter procession of poor Passover pilgrims, as an embodied representation of Jesus' Reign of God movement, was a clear ideological and political challenge to Roman imperial rule. The meaning of Jesus' grassroots procession and the arrival of the Reign of God movement during Passover could not have been clearer.

In the field of community organizing there is a well-known axiom attributed to Saul Alinsky which is that *the action is in the reaction*. Public actions and demonstrations are intended to goad and provoke an authority figure into a reaction. The reaction becomes a dynamic response that can be strategically utilized as a point of leverage. In light of the bold and direct nature of Jesus' counter procession and the clearly provocative message it was intended to send to a now irate Pilate, we must ask ourselves the question: Why is Jesus not dead by the evening of Palm Sunday?

Monday (11:12-19). On this day, Jesus performs a second demonstration and this time it is against high-priestly collaboration with Romanization. The prophet Jeremiah had warned the people that God would destroy the Temple if they continued using Temple-fidelity as an escape-house after Torah-infidelity (Jeremiah 7:1-11), and he had almost died for it (Jeremiah 26:1-24). Jesus fulfils that threat symbolically by overturning the Temple's fiscal support and disrupting its sacrificial practices.

This second demonstration, now focused on the complicit role of the high priests in the Romanization of the Temple, should be understood as an escalation from the first action the prior day. Historically, organizers, leaders and movements have at times made the strategic and tactical choice to organize not just one demonstration, but a succession of escalating demonstrations. There are a series of reasons for planning and executing consecutive, escalating, and direct nonviolent actions.

For one, it is an effective manner of generating momentum amongst the grassroots base. Within this particular context, during Passover when thousands were gathered in Jerusalem, what better time and place for Jesus and his Reign of God movement to build momentum from one day to the next by following the nonviolent counter procession into Jerusalem on Sunday by carrying out their Temple demonstration on Monday? Surely, the counter procession on Sunday would have been the "talk of the Temple" on Sunday and early Monday. For the many who participated in the counter procession and for the many who witnessed it, there must have been a sense of excitement and anticipation of what would come next.

Another reason for holding consecutive demonstrations one right after another is to advance a clear message from the people to the opposition. The first counter procession was a direct challenge to Pontius Pilate, the Roman Imperial regime and their ideological conviction that peace would be attained through violence and victory. The message of Jesus' nonviolent Reign of God procession that peace was only achievable through justice was modeled quite illustratively through the procession of poor people marching peacefully as Jesus sat atop a commonplace donkey.

The flipping of the money tables and abrupt disruption of the lucrative flow of sacrifices and exchanges in the Temple, as the second of Jesus'

Passover demonstrations, was a bold denunciation of co-optation of the Temple by the Roman Empire, its local authorities, and the high priests. The overarching message conveyed through these two escalating actions made it very clear that the unholy alliance between the Roman Empire, the high-priestly class and the economic elites was destructive and death-dealing. It was anathema to God's vision for the world, and Jesus' Reign of God movement stood in direct opposition to it.

Another reason why consecutive escalating actions are carried out is to pursue a tactically courageous and bold path that leaves the oppressor little time to regain their footing and balance. The impact of each successive action and demonstration heightens the possibility that the oppressor will make a strategic blunder in their response. When you want to goad the opposition into making a tactical mistake and public blunder, you direct your energies towards the resources and elements they value most.

As a representative of the Roman Empire, Pontius Pilate's primary responsibility was to "keep the peace" and maintain the false facade of security and stability within Jerusalem and across his assigned territories. Few things could quite as effectively and swiftly disrupt the steady flow of taxes and tributes to Rome as civil uprisings and protracted violent conflict. Taxes and tributes were mercilessly and relentlessly collected across all facets of the local economy, including from the financial activity that flowed through the Temple. Such money would have been at its zenith during Passover, thus making Jesus' overturning of the tables and halting of commercial activity all the more audacious and effective as a disruptive nonviolent action.

This is something Jesus and his people would have certainly understood given the high stakes of the moment during Passover. Saul Alinsky referred to this type of strategic thinking as "political jujitsu." In jujitsu, you focus on your opponent's center of gravity and use that to destabilize them. In community organizing, more politically astute and experienced organizers and organizations seek out points of vulnerability such as an arrogant personality, a hypocritical stance on taxes and crime, a greed-filled obsession with a polluting factory, or a quick temper, then relentlessly exploit those weaknesses and further exposing them. Their center of gravity or vulnerability becomes a point of leverage that can be exposed to the detriment of the oppressor.

Inevitably, these disruptive demonstrations were carried out with the understanding that they were going to provoke a strong and swift reaction from Pilate and the high-priests. After all, Jesus' actions were directly focused on the things they most prized: order, fear, submission, the maintenance of the status quo, and the continual flow of money and goods. The pressure and stakes surrounding Jesus would have been unbearably high. So why, we ask again, is he not dead by Monday evening?

The answer from Mark is "when the chief priests and the scribes heard it [that is, Jesus quoting Jeremiah 7:11], they kept looking for a way to kill him; for they were afraid of him, because the whole crowd was spellbound by his teaching" (11:18). The rather vague "many people ... others" of Sunday is now "the whole crowd." We begin to see that, if Jesus is protected by his supporters in Bethany's village by night, he is also protected by his supporters in Jerusalem's Temple by day.

Tuesday (11:20-13:37). That protection-by-"crowd" continues and increases on this day. The Temple authorities debate on five different subjects with Jesus and, against their lethally dangerous opposition, it is the "crowd" that protects Jesus, and does so three times.

43

First, Jesus debates with "the chief priests, the scribes, and the elders" about John the Baptist. The result is "they were afraid of the crowd, for all regarded John as truly a prophet" (11:32).

Second, Jesus tells the parable of the Rebel Tenants. Afterwards, "when they [those "chief priests, the scribes, and the elders" from 11:27] realized that he had told this parable against them, they wanted to arrest him, but they feared the crowd. So they left him and went away" (12:12).

Third, "scribes" receive both positive (12:28-34) and negative (12:38-40) reactions from Jesus. In between, when Jesus questions their teaching on the Messiah as Son of David, "the large crowd was listening to him with delight" (12:37).

Wednesday (14:1-11). All of that protection-by-"crowd" from and against chief-priestly collaboration with Rome (Caiaphas with Pilate!) is now formally confirmed: "It was two days before the Passover and the festival of Unleavened Bread. The chief priests and the scribes were looking for a way to arrest Jesus by stealth and kill him; for they said, 'Not during the festival, or there may be a riot among the people'" (14:1-2).

At that point, Jesus is safe. Even after that double and very public demonstration, his daily protective screen by the "crowd" has been successful. So what happened to change that outcome? For all the supporters who surrounded Jesus and protected him, there would have been Roman collaborators within his circle and movement who would have felt pressure to betray his trust and the movement.

In Mark's account, it was Judas' betrayal that allowed "a crowd with swords and clubs, from the chief priests, the scribes, and the elders" (14:43) to gain that desired arrest by stealth during darkness in Gethsemane. That was exactly the place to intercept Jesus before he continued north or south around the Mount of Olives to safety at Bethany.

Jesus' movement was not the first nor was it the last movement to be undermined by internal figures who were co-opted by the oppressor. In more modern times, it is widely known that J. Edgar Hoover of the FBI had identified informants who were close to Dr. King and involved in the Civil Rights Movement who played a role in Hoover's relentless campaign to "discredit, disrupt and destroy" the standing of the movement and Dr. King himself.

The FBI had also infiltrated the Black Panthers and had targeted Fred Hampton who they had internally labeled a "messiah" figure. Because of his ability as a leader to unite people across racial lines and his growing grassroots power, Hampton was seen as a threat. Using detailed information about Hampton's apartment layout that the FBI had obtained from their informant, William O'Neal, who served as Hampton's security chief, the FBI planned the raid with the Chicago police which led to Hampton's death. He was shot in the head twice at close range while he was asleep.

At the age of eighteen, William O'Neal was offered a deal by FBI agent Roy Martin Mitchell. O'Neal had been caught driving a stolen car across state lines and in order to have his felony charges dropped and to avoid jail time, he agreed to infiltrate the Black Panthers as an informant. O'Neal's counterintelligence work was part of the FBI's larger COINTELPRO operation to discredit civil rights organizations and leaders.

The FBI secured many of its informants through coercion, threat, and intimidation. Powerful nations and empires have long sought to destroy, undermine and discredit grassroots movements through various forms of external (campaigns of military and police force) and internal (campaigns of deception, discreditation and co-optation) pressures. Many people who are poor and desperate within these nations and societies who end up entangled in the webs of law enforcement agencies are vulnerable to the kind of pressure tactics that the FBI exerted on an eighteen-year-old William O'Neal. In 2021, a film titled "Judas and the Black Messiah" was released to national audiences. It depicts the FBI's intent and O'Neal's role in infiltrating the Black Panthers and Fred Hampton's inner circle. As the title of the film suggests, the biblical story of Judas' betrayal of Jesus and his movement, whether historically accurate or not, continues to be a relevant symbol for the ways in which social movements, grassroots organizations and its leaders are targeted by the powerful through means of highly sophisticated intelligence, manipulation, coercion and co-optation.

Another contemporary example of this was the Polish Solidarity (Solidarnósc) movement, which struggled with its own internal challenges with members and supporters who were working covertly on behalf of Poland's own communist security services (SB) with support, direction and influence from the Soviet KGB. At the time, the Soviets viewed the Solidarity movement as an existential threat to their control across the

Eastern Bloc in that it could lead to uprisings and destabilize communist rule in other Soviet controlled nations. As movements gain influence and momentum, there is always the risk of internal disputes and splintering as well as covert efforts by the oppressor to intimidate, threaten and manipulate grassroots leaders in order to destroy a movement and its central leadership from the inside.

What is clear is that Jesus posed a significant threat to the Roman Imperial establishment in Jerusalem and as previously in Galilee. He was a beloved figure to many poor and dispossessed people across Galilee. His popularity, moral and spiritual gravity, and authority only continued to grow the more his Reign of God movement expanded. As that reputation increased, his teachings, encounters, and actions further threatened Roman authority and exposed its collaboration with the Jewish religious hierarchy.

Jesus' double demonstrations, filled with prophetic meaning, tactical brilliance and bold proclamations, were culminating events that galvanized supporters of his movement and drew the ire of the Roman and Jewish authorities. Despite the sizable crowd that protected him, there were vulnerabilities given the constant surveillance of Jesus by the authorities. Even the cover of protection that Jesus' supporters offered could not fully shield him from the reaction and determination of Rome.

Also, *the* weak point in Jesus' protection program was precisely Gethsemane as the transition-location between day-security and night-security, between the crowd in Jerusalem and the family in Bethany. If arrested there at night, he could be crucified swiftly before the protecting crowd could intervene or maybe even knew about it.

The Rejecting Crowd

From Sunday to Wednesday of Mark's Holy Week, as we have just seen, Jesus' supportive and protective screen is first named as "many ... and others" (*polloi ... kai alloi*) in 11:8, then, more regularly, as "the crowd" (*ho ochlos*) in 11:18,32; 12:12, 37), and finally as "the people" (*ho laos*) in 14:2. That is Jesus' protecting "crowd."

Then comes Jesus' rejecting "crowd." Here is how Mark, our first account of what happened and major source of the other versions, describes its arrival before Pilate:

At the festival he used to release a prisoner for them, anyone for whom they asked. Now a man called Barabbas was in prison with the rebels who had committed murder during the insurrection. So the crowd (*ochlos*) came and began to ask Pilate to do for them according to his custom. (15:6-8)

Pilate offers them Jesus instead of Barabbas but "the chief priests stirred up the crowd (*ochlos*) to have him release Barabbas for them instead" (15:11). As Pilate continues to ask about Jesus, "they shouted" and "they shouted all the more" that he should "Crucify him"! (15:13-14). Finally, "Pilate, wishing to satisfy the crowd (*ochlos*), released Barabbas for them; and after flogging Jesus, he handed him over to be crucified" (15:15). That account raises two questions: One rather obvious, the other not so obvious but much more basic.

The obvious question is this: How does the protecting crowd that began by twice shouting "Blessed" *for* Jesus on Palm Sunday (11:9-10) relate to that rejecting crowd that twice shouted "Crucify" *against* Jesus on Good Friday (15:13-14)? Is there only one crowd, and rather fickle? Or are there two crowds, and quite distinct?

There is, however, an even more foundational question: Is that story about Barabbas and the rejecting "crowd" an historical incident about Jesus *or* a parabolic creation by Mark? Four points persuade us that Mark intended and created that scenario of Barabbas *versus* Jesus as a very deliberate parable. In short, *Paschal Barabbas* is as fictional a character as the *Good Samaritan* or the *Prodigal Son*.

Crowd-chosen Amnesty? No authority—ancient or modern—would ever have established such an amnesty, would allow "the crowd" to get freedom for "anyone for whom they asked." An annual festival amnesty for a prisoner or prisoners chosen by autocratic or administrative authority, maybe, but not one chosen by "the crowd" itself.

Special Festival Amnesty? If crowd-chosen amnesty is impossible for Roman law, what about governor-chosen amnesty? Almost impossible—for Pilate! In his attack-treatise *Against Flaccus* (=AF), governor of Egypt (33-38 CE), Philo of Alexandria imagines the greatest Roman imperial celebration, namely "the famous festival and assembly in honor of the birthday of the illustrious emperor ... the natal festival of a good emperor."

He then asks what might a Roman governor do about criminal executions with that celebration pending? Here are Philo's two best scenarios.

One scenario was postponement of the execution. A good governor would "delay the execution" of even those who "had committed the most countless iniquities" and had "been lawfully condemned" until after the festival (*AF* 80).

The other scenario was deposition after crucifixion. "I have known instances before now of men who have been crucified when this festival and assembly was at hand, being taken down and given up to their relatives, in order to receive the honours of sepulture" (*AF* 83). You will notice that Philo cannot even imagine a governor-chosen festival amnesty, that is, an "entire forgiveness," but only "a brief and temporary respite from punishment" (*AF* 84).

Mark's Parabolic Purpose? Why does Mark create such a parable, about what, and for whom? Mark is writing after the destruction of Jerusalem and its Temple in 70 CE. He explains why that happened in prophetic symbolism from 30 CE. Jerusalem, he says, chose the wrong savior, the violent son-of-the father, the false *barabbas*, rather than the nonviolent Son-of-the Father, the true *BarAbbas*. Indeed, that very name is Mark's rather clear indication that this is a parable since the equivalent of *Fatherson* is not very helpful to distinguish one male from another.

Roman Justice Caricatured. Mark gets a second benefit from inventing that parable about an annual crowd-chosen paschal amnesty. It is not the benefit of indicting the crowd and the Jews but of caricaturing Pilate and the Romans. By expanding his parable from "the crowd" coming for Barabbas (15:6-8) to "the crowd" shouting against Jesus (15:9-15), Mark ridicules Pilate as a hypocritical coward who allows them to dictate his decision. He thereby lowers the court to the arena where the shouting crowd's upward thumbs could save a fallen gladiator even against the emperor's own downward thumb. But arena-tumult is not court-protocol and what an emperor might tolerate, a judge would not. Pilate is a calculated parody of Rome's vaunted law, a satire on its boasted justice, a lampoon of its acclaimed civilization. In other words, Mark's parable is intended to be a stinging and comical rebuke of Rome and Pilate's authority in a manner that cleverly and simultaneously diminishes their standing and legitimacy and raises "the crowd" of poor and destitute people to equal if not greater footing than the Empire.

In summary, Mark's Holy Week has a single *historical* "crowd" protecting Jesus from Sunday through Wednesday. That other "crowd" is not historical but *parabolical* and Mark's creation symbolizes in Barabbas over Jesus in 30 CE the fateful choice of *violent* over *nonviolent* resistance in 70 CE (15:6-8). It also ridicules the judgment of Pilate and lampoons the justice of Rome (15:9-15). Mark was essentially using political humor to accentuate this point.

Historically, political humor has been leveraged and used as an effective organizing tactic by those who are oppressed in order to gain a psychological advantage against their oppressor. One reason for lampooning one's oppressor and their dehumanizing nature is that it serves to diminish the aura of invisibility and inevitability of the oppressor. Songs, chants, artistic murals, posters, picket signs, theatrical plays, satirical cartoons and social media memes have all been used to discredit, delegitimize and diminish the illusion of absolute power that the powerful and mighty have always sought to maintain.

Freedom Riders used songs and chants to point out the obvious lunacy of Jim Crow laws and practices and the obsessive compulsiveness with maintaining them. Satirical memes and cartoons were deployed effectively against the Murabak regime during the 2011 Egyptian Revolution. Saul Alinsky, one of the founders of church and institution-based organizing, wrote extensively about the use of humor as one of the tools that the oppressed have at their disposal to weaken an opponent's authority by exposing their ridiculous attitudes, fragile egos and deep contradictions.

Jesus in Jerusalem that Passover

If we ask why Jesus went to Jerusalem that Passover, our best answer is because he was invited there by sympathizers and supporters of his vision for God's Reign on Earth. Time and time again, Dr. King and the Southern Christian Leadership Conference (SCLC) leaders were urged by their supporters across the U.S. to organize desegregation campaigns in their cities and towns. The Rev. Fred Shuttlesworth famously persuaded the SCLC to launch a desegregation campaign in Birmingham, Alabama or "Bombingham" as it was then notoriously called.

Several years later in 1968, King's deep fidelity to those who were amongst the most poor and exploited is what led him to travel to Memphis, Tennessee to support African-American sanitation workers who were on strike for more dignified treatment and better pay. During his second visit to Memphis in April of that year King's life was tragically cut short by an assassin's bullet. Several from his inner circle pleaded with him to avoid this trip, and yet King accepted the invitation. The plight and courageous struggle of the sanitation workers struck a deep chord with King despite the inherent risk that traveling to Memphis posed.

One can imagine Jesus weighing a similar fateful choice. Prioritize his own safety and security or go to where his people were inviting him to come. Why, they might have asked, should he stay in those Galilean hamlets away from the local center of imperial power in Jerusalem? Why not come to the capital and during Passover where throngs of people would be gathered. Come for twin demonstrations: One, based on Zecharia 9, was against Roman occupation and violence; the other, based on Jeremiah 7, will be against high-priestly collaboration and injustice. Our numbers can keep you safe, in the Temple by day, and in Bethany by night.

That preceding section emphasized history, as what you should know, and parable, as what you should do (recall "go and do" in Luke 10:37). We repeat an example of each mode in conclusion to this chapter's second major section.

The historical example is from Josephus. His description of Jesus' execution in his *Jewish Antiquities*, from the 90s CE, is the most reliable factual summary of that death: "Pilate, upon hearing him accused by men of the highest amongst us ... condemned him to be crucified" (18:64). That is, literally, "the first men," and is a favorite Josephan word for "the leaders." In Jerusalem it would include but not specify the high priests, nothing is said there, however, about any influence from the crowd or the people.

The parabolical example is from John who creates this answer from Jesus to Pilate during his imaginary interrogation: "My kingdom is not from this world. If my kingdom were from this world, my followers would be fighting to keep me from being handed over ... But as it is, my kingdom is not from here." (18:36). The Reign of Rome, like all earthly kingdoms, is based on violence and protected by it. The Reign of God is a heavenly kingdom on this earth, but does not use violence even to liberate Jesus.

That claim raises these preparatory problems as we face this chapter's third and final major question. Did Jesus' movement involve nonviolence (passive) or nonviolent resistance (active)? In either case, was he inventing a strategy or participating in one already created and practiced before him?

THE REIGN OF GOD AND NONVIOLENT RESISTANCE

How did Jewish leaders interact with the Romanization of Judea and Galilee in the first-century? Were they all and always collaborators? Did some of them support violent revolt? Did some of them *invent* programmatic large-scale nonviolent resistance? If so, was that the immediate matrix for the nonviolent resistance of John's Jordan-Baptism movement and Jesus' Divine-Reign movement? If Jesus ended his life on a Roman cross, did that prove him, at least from Pilate's judgment, to be a violent rebel or a nonviolent resister?

Violent Resistance to Romanization

We know that there were four *violent* Jewish revolts against Roman power in the first 200 years of imperial control: Three times in the homeland (4 BCE, 66-73 CE, 132-135 CE); and once both inside and outside it (115-117 CE). Our major source for those first two violent revolts is, of course, Josephus whose *Jewish War* and *Jewish Antiquities* we have met repeatedly in this book.

Josephus also wrote an autobiography in which he claimed priestly descent through his father and royal descent through his mother. Next, at age fourteen, "the chief priests and the leading men of the city used to constantly come to me for precise information on some particular in our ordinances." Then, at nineteen, he chose "to govern my life by the rules of the Pharisees." Finally, at twenty-six, he was sent to a high-profile embassy to defend some accused priests before Nero. After surviving a shipwreck, he succeeded in that defense, and also "received large gifts from Poppaea," Nero's wife (*Life* 1-15; Luke may have known and used Josephus).

That Roman visit was in 61. At the start of the Judeo-Roman war of 66-73 CE, the Jerusalem leadership appointed Josephus to organize and defend rebel Galilee. Defeated and captured there by Rome's avenging legions, he prophesied, possibly from that very victory, that their leader; Vespasian would be Rome's next emperor. When that became true in 69 CE by on-site acclamation of those same avenging legions around Jerusalem, Josephus became a client of the new Flavian dynasty for whom he wrote a Roman defense of their *Jewish War*. That defense had two fundamental themes.

The first theme concerned the Romans. Josephus claimed that: God gave world power to the Roman Empire (*JW* 5.367; *JA* 2.390); God gave Roman power to the Flavian dynasty (JW 4.622; 5.1); and God gave Flavian power to Vespasian who was, in fact, the awaited Messiah *from* Judea. That Messiah or world conqueror was not, as mistakenly expected, a Jew in Judea by birth but a Roman in Judea by conquest (*JW* 6.312-313). Therefore, for Jews to rebel against Rome was to rebel against God just as rebellions by colonized people against their French, British and American colonial oppressors was regarded as a rebellion against God's will.

The second theme concerned the Jews. Josephus claimed that the three main Jewish leadership groups, the Essenes, Pharisees, and Sadducees, were not religio-political factions dangerous to Rome, but "three philosophies" in no way threatening to Roman occupation of the Jewish homeland (*JW* 2.119–166; *JA* 18:11-12).

Behind or beneath Josephus' religio-political propaganda in the 70s, be it defending Romans against Jews or Jews against Romans, was one great abiding fear. Jewish adult males paid an annual tax, the equivalent of two days' wages for a laborer, to support Jerusalem's Temple. After Rome had destroyed that Temple in 70, and as a punishment for the war in which it happened, Rome enlarged that tax to *every* Jewish person and diverted it to the support of its own Capitoline Temple to Jupiter Optimus Maximus.

For Josephus, therefore, the fearful or even appalling thought was *what if* Rome judged Judaism to be theologically inimical to Rome and decreed that its practice—for example, male circumcision—was forbidden or made effectively impossible? To assuage that fear, Josephus opposed not only violent resistance but even or especially nonviolent resistance against Romanization.

Nonviolent Resistance to Romanization

Recall from the preceding chapter, that in 4 BCE, on the death of his father Herod the Great, Archelaus became Rome's Jewish client-ruler of Samaria, Judea and Idumea. But he lasted there for less than a decade.

In 6 CE, Augustus replaced him with a Roman ruler Coponius, who was, however, subordinate to the Syrian legate Quirinius. That shift from indirect to direct Roman rule required a taxation-census not of the people but "of their property" (*JA* 18.2). The result, as we know from Luke, was that "Judas the Galilean rose up at the time of the census and got people to follow him; he also perished, and all who followed him were scattered" (Acts 5:37). But was that uprising itself violent or nonviolent? It was, according to Josephus, the start or even the invention of programmatic, large-scale, nonviolent resistance which he obfuscates in his pro-Roman 70s (*JW* 2.118) but admits, even if through gritted teeth, in his pro-Jewish 90s (*JA* 18.4-10 & 23-25).

First, Josephus eventually but reluctantly admits that, apart from those "three philosophies" just mentioned, there was also a "fourth philosophy" but he qualifies it as "an innovation and reform in ancestral traditions ... an intrusive fourth school of philosophy ... the novelty of a hitherto unknown philosophy ... the fourth of the philosophies" (*JA* 18.9, 23).

Second, he also connects this "fourth philosophy" with the Pharisees: "Judas, a Gaulanite from a city named Gamala, had enlisted the aid of Saddok a Pharisee" and, further, Judas' "school agrees in all other respects with the opinions of the Pharisees, except that ... they are convinced that God alone is their leader and master" (*JA* 18.4,23).

Third, in terms of content, the "fourth philosophy" is the theory and practice of unarmed nonviolent resistance backed up by an acceptance of potential martyrdom which, presumably, God would either prevent here or reward hereafter. Josephus, however, has absolutely no sympathy for those organized, large-scale but unarmed resisters. Instead, he rejects them, as a "body of villains with purer hands but more impious intentions" (*JW* 2.258 = *JA* 20.164). As *nonviolent* they have "purer hands" but as *resistance* they have "impious intentions."

Josephus' disdain for those who practiced nonviolent resistance is quite a far cry from Mahatma Gandhi's insistence centuries later that nonviolence is the weapon of the brave and that it is an act of supreme courage to maintain it in the face of oppression.

Finally, on the one hand, Josephus never *admits* clearly that Judas' strategy involved nonviolent resistance even, if necessary, unto martyrdom. Instead, for his pro-Roman audience, he speaks obliquely of that "fourth philosophy" expecting its followers to "stand firm and not shrink from the bloodshed [*or* burden] that might be necessary" (*JA* 18.5), bloodshed, that is, not by them but against them. Indeed, "they think little of submitting to death in unusual forms and permitting vengeance to fall on kinsmen and friends" so that no "report may minimize the indifference with which they accept the grinding misery of pain" (*JA* 18.23-24).

On the other hand, Josephus *describes* very fully such incidents of organized nonviolent resistance between its invention in 6 CE and the resumption of violent revolt in 66 CE. He mentions it, for example against Pilate in 26 CE, both for bringing iconic military standards into Jerusalem and using Temple funds for a city aqueduct (*JW* 2.169-177 = *JA* 18.55-62). There is also the even more spectacular nonviolent resistance in 40 CE against Caligula's legionary-backed attempt to put his divine statue in Jerusalem's Temple (*JW* 2.184-203 = *JA* 18.261-309).

John the Baptist and Jesus practiced nonviolent resistance against Herod Antipas' commercialization in Galilee; Jesus also used nonviolent demonstrations in Judea against both Pilate's Romanization and Caiaphas' collaboration. They both operated within the matrix of a practice *already used* in 6 CE by Judas, another Galilean, and Saddoq, presumably a Judean, against Coponius' Romanization and commercialization in Judea. (Since we have no historical evidence of any earlier use of such organized large-scale nonviolent resistance, Judas and Saddoq probably *invented* it.)

In any case, John and Jesus adopted that strategy of nonviolent resistance and gave it their own differing theological justifications. They also both died for its practice, as have many other followers of Jesus' commitment to nonviolent resistance since then such as Ken Saro-Wiwa (Nigeria), Sr. Dorothy Stang (Brazil) and Fr. Rutilio Grande (El Salvador).

HOW TO "LOVE YOUR ENEMIES"

That Jesus' Reign of God movement was both resistant and nonviolent is confirmed from Rome's history and law outside the New Testament, and from Jesus' vision and justification in the earliest stratum inside it.

From Outside the New Testament

At the end of that first century, the Jewish historian Josephus recorded: "Jesus, a wise man ... [who] won over many Jews and many of the Greeks," and, as we have already seen, "Pilate, upon hearing him accused by men of the highest standing amongst us ... condemned him to be crucified" (*JA* 18.63-64). At the start of the second century, the Roman historian Tacitus gave much the same summary: "Christus, the founder of the name, had undergone the death penalty in the reign of Tiberius, by sentence of the procurator Pontius Pilatus" (*Annals* 15.44).

You will notice that neither author says anything about executions or even arrests for Jesus' primary supporters or secondary sympathizers. There were not, twelve crosses on Calvary. That is, admittedly, an argument from silence but still it is a significant silence. Why?

For *violent* resistance, Rome crucified the leader together with his most important supporters or top commanders. In 4 BCE at Jerusalem, for example, the Syrian governor captured "the authors of the insurrection ... the most culpable, in number about two thousand, he crucified" (*JW* 2:75; *JA* 17.295). Also, of course, recall that those arrested in Mark's parable were "Barabbas ... with the rebels who had committed murder during the insurrection" (15:7).

For *nonviolent* resistance, Rome crucified only the leader on the presumption that, lacking him, the movement would soon dissipate. Here, once again, is Julius Paulus Prudentissimus on another juridical precedent in Roman law: "The authors of sedition and tumult, or those who stir up the people, shall, according to their rank, either be crucified, thrown to wild beasts, or deported to an island" (*The Opinions of Julius Paulus Addressed to His Son*, Book V, Title XXII, #1). Nothing is said about punishment for sympathizers, supporters, or even subordinate leaders.

That is why both Josephus and Tacitus thought it necessary to explain why, despite Jesus' execution for nonviolent resistance, his movement not only survived but spread all the way to Rome. For Josephus: "those who had in the first place come to love him did not give up their affection for him … And the tribe of the Christians, so called after him, has still to this day not disappeared" (*JA* 18.64). For Tacitus: "the pernicious superstition was checked for the moment, only to break out once more, not merely in Judaea, the home of the disease, but in the capital itself, where all things horrible or shameful in the world collect and find a vogue" (*Annals* 15.44).

That Jesus' movement continued to expand in the aftermath of his public execution is a testament to the profound influence of his life, teachings, and moral and spiritual vision. The women and men who accompanied Jesus during the brief tenure of his public life and ministry were vital members of a growing nonviolent movement before his death. After Jesus' violent death by torture, these women and men became vital leaders of an increasingly organized movement, something that very rarely happens after the brutal death of a charismatic and galvanizing leader. Most often, movements, organizations and their people find themselves scattered and aimless after such traumatic events.

The core convictions of Jesus' spiritual genius, rooted in a commitment to communal distribution, divine collaboration, and nonviolent resistance to imperial exploitation and oppression, was somehow sustained and nurtured by a small group of poor peasants in the cauldron of the Roman Empire. It speaks to something that organizers and leaders have painstakingly struggled to accomplish throughout history, which is how to inspire people to not only believe in a morally audacious vision and future, but to believe so fervently in themselves and in their calling and ability to make a meaningful contribution that they dedicate their lives to it.

From Inside the New Testament

Appropriately and climatically, we conclude this chapter with the most striking command ever given by Jesus. It is: "love your enemies" and is contained in the *Gospel according to Q which, along with the Gospel according to Mark,* was one of the two major sources used by Matthew and Luke. Also in Greek, that "your" is plural rather than singular and communal rather than individual.

In Leviticus, the Torah had commanded the Israelites to "love your neighbor as yourself" and to "love the resident alien as yourself" (19:18,34). That *love of neighbors* is cited in the New Testament by Jesus in Mark 12:3, by Paul in Galatians 5:14 and Romans 13:9, and by James 2:8. That *love of immigrants* is, then and now, most difficult but, surely, *love of enemies* is almost impossible.

Those enemies are not ones who annoy, oppose, criticize, or even humiliate you. That startling command is accompanied by parallel ones indicating "enemies" as those who persecute, hate, curse, and abuse you— and persecutors are often killers (Luke 11:49; *Acts* 7:52; 22:4). Those parallels concern life-threatening enmity: "love your enemies, pray for those who persecute you (Matthew 5:44); "love your enemies, do good to those who hate you, bless those who curse you, pray for those who abuse you ... love your enemies (Luke 6:27-28,35).

The questions about Jesus' "love your enemies" are rather obvious. First, why did Jesus not just say to love everyone, why specify enemies, why presume that his hearers could always find enemies, would always confront enemies, should always love enemies? Next, after two thousand years of Christian history is that love-commandment as fatuous as it is famous and as vacuous in practice as it is virtuous in theory? Finally, does "love your enemies" enable violence, cooperate with violence, and at least suggest indifference to violence?

We remind you that our term *nonviolent resistance* never appears as a command on the lips of Jesus, nor anywhere else in the New Testament. Instead, the historical Jesus commands *love of enemies*. That was his own succinct way of advocating the justice of nonviolent resistance (*love*) against the injustice of violent oppression from others (*your enemies*). Love of enemies is embodied in, practiced by, and identified with nonviolent resistance to them. Roman authorities did not execute—and their official Jewish collaborators did not accuse—leaders who advocated "love your enemies" but they did remove leaders who organized nonviolent resistance against them!

Also, and crucially, Jesus not only gave "love your enemies" as his succinct summary and programmatic mantra for nonviolent resistance, he also gave this reason for accepting it: "for God makes his sun rise on the evil (*ponērous*) and on the good" in Matthew 5:45, and "God is kind to the ungrateful and the evil (*ponērous*)" in Luke 6:35.

The basic empowerment for nonviolent resistance on the human level is that human nonviolent resistance participates in divine nonviolent resistance. That was/is the transcendental vision of John's parable about Jesus before Pilate where Jesus explicitly incarnates the nonviolent Reign of God and Pilate implicitly incarnates the violent Reign of Rome (John 18:36). That was/is Jesus' visionary empowerment for Passover in Jerusalem. That was/is Jesus' challenge claiming only nonviolent resistance can confront violence without enabling its escalatory spiral. That was/is what God revealed to humanity by the nonviolent Jesus' violent execution but "none of the rulers of this age understood this; for if they had, they would not have crucified the Lord of glory" (1 Corinthians 2:8).

Legacy of Nonviolent Resistance

Jesus' abiding commitment to nonviolent resistance and loving one's enemies represents a stunning example with profound theological insights into the will of God that many others have followed since. Although Jesus was not the first to invent nonviolent resistance, as we explored earlier in this chapter, his unique combination of an anti-imperial divine vision (Reign of God), countercultural teachings (love your enemies) and nonviolent prophetic actions (counter procession and temple demonstration) represent a singular example of spiritual genius, moral courage, and divine wisdom that has inspired countless people and movements throughout history since his public execution.

Mahatma Gandhi drew his inspiration from Jesus and his Sermon on the Mount for the critical moral, spiritual, and theological insights that led to the development of the nonviolence philosophy and practice of *Satyagraha (love force)*. Gandhi's belief that love was an active and dynamic force capable of transforming both people and societies can be traced back to his insightful understanding of Jesus' application of love and nonviolent resistance as a moral and spiritual force vital in liberating India from British colonial rule. Years later, Martin Luther King, Jr. would apply many of these same philosophical, theological and strategic insights of nonviolent resistance in the struggle against the evils of racism, militarism and greed in the United States.

In addition to Gandhi and King, Jesus' teachings and commitment to nonviolent resistance has inspired countless others. Those include: Dorothy

Day, founder of the Catholic Worker; Baynard Rustin, famed civil rights organizer and mentor to Dr. King; Dolores Huerta co-founder of the United Farm Workers; and Rev. James Lawson, leading supporter, tactician and theoretician of nonviolence during the civil rights movement. In addition to these important historical figures, many others gave their lives in the midst of nonviolent struggles for peace and justice. Saint Oscar Romero was assassinated for defending the rights of his people and challenging his government's atrocities and violations of human rights. Sister Dorothy Stang was brutally murdered for defending the Amazon rainforests and their poor farmers against criminal gangs and powerful ranchers who colluded to steal and deforest indigenous lands.

Jesus' life, teachings and commitment to nonviolent resistance continue to be a source of inspiration to countless people and organizations who are working for justice and peace across the world today. By illuminating the social and political context in which Jesus preached, healed, mobilized poor and destitute people, and engaged in acts of nonviolent resistance, we are able to appreciate the depth of his courage and spiritual genius. The rising tide of violence, hatred, racism, greed and authoritarianism in our world today can only be met with a greater *power* of love, courage, compassion and nonviolent resistance if we wish to follow Jesus' footsteps in working to achieve a greater approximation of God's Reign on Earth.

CHAPTER 3

THE RESURRECTION OF JESUS

Christ has risen! This message is proclaimed in places of worship across the world every Easter Sunday. Pastors preach of Christ's resurrection from the dead as a pinnacle moment in the dramatic arc of Jesus' short life on earth. Each year millions of Christians mark Easter Sunday with food, music, and celebration. Churches are adorned with decor; parish pews are filled with people; parks and yards are filled with billowing smoke from barbecue grills; and children frantically search for candy-filled eggs. In many places, it is a day that is far more preoccupied with superficial celebrations and theological proclamations than it is with honest reflection and quiet discernment on the path that Jesus' resurrection beckons us to walk.

The miracle of the resurrection is a central tenet of Christian faith. This miracle and world altering moment is meant to guide and shape the convictions, actions and commitments of Christians around the world. Beyond the superficial celebrations and empty theological proclamations lies the deeper and often unexplored question of what the story of the resurrection meant to early Christian communities and how this can inform our understanding of the resurrection today. A clearer and more historically rooted understanding of the resurrection is a vital element of the broader challenge of recovering the historical Jesus from our dominant cultural context in order to discern the profound moral and spiritual genius that his life, execution, and resurrection has to teach us.

Deeper exploration of the resurrection question within the context of Roman imperial domination and Jesus' nonviolent Reign of God movement can shed light on the universally life-affirming, and consequently anti-imperial, implications of the resurrection. Through their decision to publicly execute Jesus, Pontius Pilate and the Roman Empire were determined to decimate and scatter Jesus' Reign of God movement. Any criticism of and public agitation against the Roman Empire's political and economic order in first-century Palestine along with its co-optation of the Temple and high priests could not be tolerated. Rome believed that any movement directed toward upending its dominant control either violently or nonviolently, would die on the vine with its leaders and co-conspirators cut at the root and hung on the cross.

Therefore, can it be that the story of Jesus' resurrection developed, shaped and widely proclaimed by Jesus' followers had an intended message for early Christian communities *and* the Roman Empire? Perhaps the original meaning of the resurrection story was meant to inspire and challenge, invoke and provoke, and encourage and disrupt? Of course, these questions lead to other questions: How did early Christians come to develop images and thus theological interpretations of the resurrection? Were there differences in interpretation that eventually developed between various Christian groups? How has this shaped our contemporary understanding of the resurrection?

Within and beyond these questions are critical historical and theological insights that can help to guide our own attempts to discern and interpret what the resurrection means for us today in light of the multitude of social, political, economic, and environmental crises we face. Rather than being a day of pastel-colored eggs and barbeques, we contend that the story of the resurrection is meant to prompt deep interior reflection and conversion that leads to courageous prophetic protagonism in pursuit of God's universal justice.

Tragically, Easter marks yet another event in the Christian liturgical calendar that has been largely co-opted by our dominant cultural forces of consumerism, nationalism, and individualism. Just as the significance and meaning of Jesus' birth as the son of two poor and desperately frightened refugee parents has been stripped from the Christmas season, the revolutionary and anti-imperial nature of Jesus' resurrection is tragically absent from the mainstream narration of the Easter story.

The resurrection story, as with the broader Gospel message of justice and compassion, remains largely captive to the dominant cultural forces of individualism, nationalism, capitalism, racism, and militarism. As such, the resurrection story itself is often understood and interpreted through a hyper individualistic lens that bears little or no resemblance to the highly communal, cultural, and religious context in which Jesus and his followers lived. Without a proper rootedness within its appropriate historical context, the resurrection message is barren of power to stir, agitate, and inspire. Resurrection therefore loses its meaning and transformative ability and is no longer a challenge to embrace a process of conversion which, both individual and universal, holds profound cosmic possibilities and implications for all of God's creation.

In the next sections, we give an in-depth historical context to show how the Christian tradition arrived at the theology and imagery of Easter and the resurrection. We begin with what we call "The Great Omission." Next, we see how that opening allowed not one but two very distinctive Easter visions. Finally, we consider how that divergence between the Easter tradition of Western Christianity as compared to Eastern Christianity presents a profound moral and spiritual challenge for our Christian response.

HOW TO IMAGINE EASTER SUNDAY?

Think about that first Easter Sunday morning as told across all four gospel versions. Notice what is present and repeated but especially what is absent and unnoticed.

We have gospel texts for the single event of the *Tomb Tradition*. That story about Jesus' first female followers and then his male ones finding the tomb empty was given in Mark 16:1-8, then copied into Matthew 28:1-7, Luke 24:1-8, and John 20:1-5, before a final expansion in post-Mark 16:9-18.

We also have gospel texts for the multiple events of the *Vision Tradition* which are those stories about Jesus' first female followers and then his male ones seeing visionary apparitions of him. We have post-mortem apparitions of Jesus in Paul (1 Corinthians 15:5-8); Matthew (28:9-10,16-20); Luke (24:13-49); and John (20:11-29; 21:1-25).

THE GREAT OMISSION

The singularity of the Tomb Tradition and the multiplicity of the Vision Tradition are so compelling that, rightly captivated by what is present, we fail to see what is absent. We may not even notice The Great Omission, which is the lack of any description of the Resurrection-*moment*, the Easter instant, the Paschal exaltation as such and in itself. But here is its challenge now, loud and clear: The major events in the life of Jesus the Messiah/Christ are described by the evangelists and granted the necessary skill, can be depicted creatively by artists. All are described except the most crucial, most climactic, most important one of them all, namely, the Resurrection-*moment* itself, the Easter transition of Jesus from inside to outside that tomb. It is as if the gospel-accounts described Jesus' Execution with the Burial but not the Crucifixion, with the Tomb but not the Cross. That lack of any description of the Resurrection-event is what we mean by The Great Omission.

That Great Omission was too glaring a lacuna not to generate both theological descriptions and—eventually—iconographical depictions as a remedy. In fact, Christianity's first millennium filled the omission with two quite divergent visions of that Easter moment; either of which or some combination of both might have become the normative Easter image. But, in its second millennium and after the Great East-West Schism of 1054, those divergent visions became, as we shall see, rather opposing options.

As we proceed, keep these two questions in mind: What is at stake in that West/East divergence of Easter theology for Christian faith and life; and would Christianity's present and future be better with some integration of both Easter visions? The following section will highlight an example of that Easter divergence, explore how it began, and, lastly, ask why it matters for Christian integrity today.

TWO IMAGES OF THE EASTER MOMENT

In the Troodos Mountains of Cyprus, ten magnificently frescoed churches, that date from the 11th to the 16th century, form the largest concentration of Byzantine murals extant anywhere and, accordingly, those village and monastic churches have been listed together as a World Heritage Site. Cyprus is, by the way, a good place to use in this chapter since it was to that island Barnabas and Paul brought the first mission *westward* from the Levantine coast in Acts 13:4-12.

Use your imagination to visit a small A-roofed church dedicated to both the All-Holy Mother of God (*Panagia Theotokos*) and the Archangel Michael located just outside the village of Galata in the Troodos' Solea Valley. As scenes from Jesus' life flow in fully-colored sequence all around the walls, it is easy to recognize the classic gospel events from Annunciation, Nativity, and Presentation; through Baptism, Lazarus, and Entrance; to Arrest, Crucifixion, and Deposition.

Then, immediately after that mournful deposition from the cross, and reading from left to right, those two images in *Figure 1* appear with, between them, the scene of Jesus and Mary Magdalene in the Garden (John 20:11-18). In *Figure 1* those two images are placed side-by-side to study their striking similarities and even more striking differences.

First, let's start with the similarities. In Greek, both images are entitled "The Anastasis" or, in English, "The Resurrection" with "The Resurrection of Christ" (left image) or simply "The Resurrection" (right image). Both images identify the protagonist as JESUS and CHRIST, in traditional Greek abbreviations on either side of his head. Both images show the earth split open around Jesus. Finally, and most significantly, both images show the Resurrected One as the Crucified One with the same three emphases: Jesus has a cruciform halo; has wounds on his hands and feet; and has a liturgical processional cross in his left hand.

Next, the differences. The left image shows a partially clothed Jesus emerging from an opened sarcophagus with his left leg still inside and his right leg outside. His wounded right hand is raised in a typical Byzantine blessing, but he is utterly alone, except, of course, for those sleeping guards with their vandalized faces.

The right image is utterly and radically different from the left one. Jesus is now fully and beautifully clothed and his wounded right hand grasps the limp wrist of aged Adam with ageless Eve beside him. *Humanity, that is, the entire human race is biblically embodied and traditionally symbolized in Adam-and-Eve.*

Still, although Adam-and-Eve already symbolizes everybody, unidentified others appear behind them. Then, on the other side of Jesus, we can identify John the Baptist behind David, crowned and white-bearded, alongside his son Solomon, crowned and beardless. (All of those identifications are certified from similar frescoes with names attached.)

Figure 1

In that left image Jesus is in the guarded tomb found only in Matthew (27:62-66; 28:4,11-15). In the right image he is in Hades, the place of universal death for all, emphatically not in Hell, the place of eternal punishment for some. Jesus' forceful advent—note the billowing cloak—has smashed open the gates of Hades/Death and sent their bars, bolts, and locks flying in all directions. He stands atop those double gates which are now in cruciform position as another emphasis that the Resurrected One is specifically the Crucified One. The double gates now in cruciform shape are meant to recall the Crucifixion as a symbolic challenge to the Roman Empire. Jesus' resurrection as the Crucified One is a triumph over Rome and its culture and systematization of death and suffering.

Here, then, is a first conclusion about the process of imagining Easter. Since the original moment of the Resurrection itself is never described, only its effects and consequences, the Christian tradition gives us two very different visions of Jesus' Resurrection (*Anastasis*), as shown in Figure 1.

The left image displays the Easter tradition of Western Christianity with the *Individual Resurrection* of Jesus who arises triumphant, magnificent, but utterly alone. The right image depicts the Easter tradition of Eastern Christianity with the *Universal Resurrection* of Jesus who arises triumphant, magnificent, but utterly universal. Jesus raises *all* of humanity—in biblical embodiment as Adam-and-Eve—from Hades, from the prison-house-of Death, along with himself.

If you wonder how West and East abide side-by-side on the same wall, the date tells the story. Cyprus was, of course, part, and a very, very early part of Eastern Christianity but it was ceded to the Venetians of Western Christianity in 1489 and so we have both Easter traditions on the wall of this church from the early 1500s.

That *Figure 1* certainly indicates clearly the distinction of Western *versus* Eastern Christianity on the Resurrection of Jesus the Messiah/ Christ. Still, and above all else, what are the implications of that divergence for contemporary Christians? Is a universal resurrection not simply all the individual resurrections taken together? In order to understand the great significance of these two divergences, we will unpack the *origins* of the location, model, image, and example of each Resurrection image.

THE ORIGINS OF THE INDIVIDUAL RESURRECTION

1. The Location. The first ever *image* depicting the actual moment of Jesus' Easter vindication was created in Roman Arelate (modern Arles) in southern France. Its Provençal creation and popularity dates from around 350 when Christians wanted the image of Christ's Resurrection-*moment* carved prominently on their stone coffins. But how could they have depicted on their sarcophagi what was never described in their biblical texts?

2. The Model. In image and/or motto, coinage was antiquity's best—or only—mass medium. But what coinage could be appropriate as a model for Jesus' Resurrection?

In the early 4th century, the emperor Constantine I the Great, having legislated toleration for Christianity also favored it personally because a visionary dream from God assured him of victory if he used the Christ-symbol on the battle standards of his legionary soldiers. Constantine's Christ-symbol or Christogram showed a victory-wreath around the Greek letters *Chi* or *X* and *Rho* or *P* but with the *Rho/P* superimposed on the *Chi/X* to form a monogram for CH/R or Christ (see *Figure 2*).

Constantine died in 337 but among his last coin-types from 336 was one from the imperial mint at Arles that depicted two legionary soldiers with down-pointed spears and shields at rest, standing on either side and

Figure 2

looking towards that military standard with Constantine's triumphant Christogram above the crossbar.

3. The Image. Imagine a flash of brilliance from someone now anonymous who solved that artistic demand for an image of the Resurrection-*moment* by creatively combining a biblical text *with* that imperial coin.

The biblical text told how Jesus' tomb-guards were bribed by the high-priests to deny what they had seen by claiming that the disciples had stolen Jesus' body while they slept (Matthew 28:13). "Guards" is plural, so at least two were involved, and "two guards" was the pivot between two *honor*-guards on a coin and two *tomb*-guards in a text (*Figure 2*).

Combining text with coin created the first image of the Resurrection as those two *honor*-guards with shields at rest become two *tomb*-guards with shields at rest but still on either side of the monogram-symbol of Christ's— and Constantine's—victory (*Figure 2*).

4. The Example. For our present purposes, we focus on the center of one Easter sarcophagus held in the Pio Cristiano Museum, named for Pius IX's collection of Christian antiquities, in the Vatican Museums. Dated to 360, this sarcophagus' front has five sections separated by columns and shows Jesus crowned bodily and physically to left and interrogated bodily and physically to right of the central Easter image where he is shown only symbolically (*Figure 2*).

There is a great amount of detail not to be missed in that image. In it the Cross is surmounted by the Greek letters *X/Chi* and *P/Rho* combined into the formal Christogram and surrounded by a bay laurel wreath with streamers to signify Christ's victory in Greco-Roman style. Linking Cross and Christogram, birds eat the berries of the bay laurel to symbolize Christians participating in that victory.

Below the crossbar are those two tomb-guards. They are essential to make this not just Christ's general victory but his particular Resurrection victory. The guards are seated with shields at rest, but the left guard represents *the truth* as he looks up and sees Christ's Easter triumph which he is bribed to deny; the right guard represents *the lie* as he is fast asleep and does not see the apostolic grave-robbery which he is bribed to claim (Matthew 28:11-15).

For the rest of Western tradition, two or more guards will appear and reappear, sometimes with all of them seeing the Resurrection-*moment*, sometimes with all of them sleeping through it, and sometimes split between the truth of seeing and the lie of sleeping.

In that first-ever image of the Resurrection-*moment*, Jesus is *not depicted physically but symbolically*. That lack of Jesus' bodily representation in the central scene contrasts forcibly with his bodily presence in the ones on either side. Indeed, all others, including those two tomb-guards, are also shown with bodily images.

Lacking a *bodily* image of Jesus, this first Western image of the Resurrection-*moment* both solved the *First Great Omission* and created a *Second Great Omission* of its own. In round numbers, the West took from the year 500 to the year 900 to solve that second omission and depict Jesus' Resurrection-*moment* with a physical rather than a symbolic image. As we see next, the East had already developed a bodily image of Jesus'

Figure 3

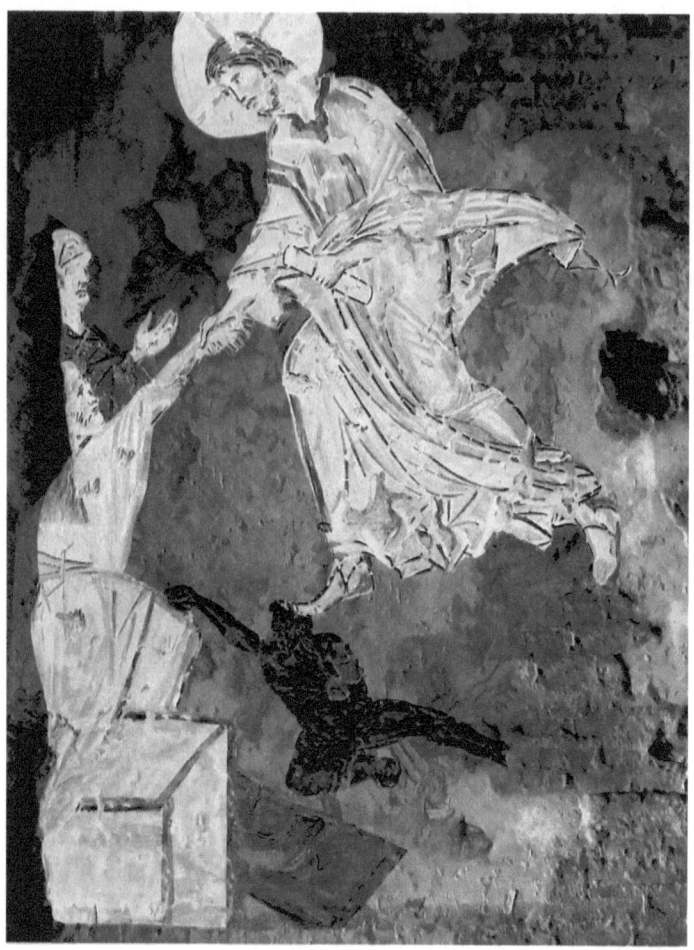

Resurrection-*moment* by the year 700 and it was a very different one than the West would eventually produce by the year 900.

In the next section, we see the difference in location, model, image and example for the origins of that Universal Resurrection. Resurrection must always be imagined and depicted physically because it is about cosmic justice which is about humanity and all of creation—as physical reality.

THE ORIGINS OF THE UNIVERSAL RESURRECTION

1. The Location. We now turn from France to Italy, Provence to Rome, and between 350 and 400 to between 705 and 707. Those latter dates are the brief reign of Pope John VII who was genetically and culturally a Byzantine or Eastern Christian.

2. The Model. Once again, the most obviously available model is from coinage depicting imperial victory. Think, however, of two such coin-types from Christian emperors. One is the ancient and brutal image of *trampling down* the conquered enemy by an imperial foot on a prostrate body. The other is the idyllic and propaganda image of *raising up* the kneeling enemy with a right-hand to right-hand grasp of friendship—conquest as liberation.

3. The Image. The original Eastern image of the Resurrection was probably from Constantinople around 675 but all its earliest extant images are from Pope John VII in 705-707. In other words, the Eastern image of Easter came around 325 years after the Western one. In any case, the original Easter image in Eastern Christianity combined those two models of imperial victory to produce a scenario of both *trampling down* one protagonist and *raising up* another.

4. The Example. For here and now, we choose as our example the Easter image from inside Pope John's papal chapel known today as the *Church of Santa Maria Antiqua* in the Roman Forum (*Figure 3*).

In this image's fourfold scenario of trampling down and *raising up*, the first and dominant character is Jesus the Messiah/Christ. With billowing garments, he comes forcibly downward from viewer right. His halo is, as always, cruciform, but here his right hand holds a scroll indicating philosophical wisdom. As you recall from *Figure 1* (right) this image's development will insist in four different ways that this was, is, and ever will be the Resurrection *of the Crucified One*.

The second character is Adam. Jesus' right hand grasps the limp wrist of Adam and takes him from his sepulcher. Adam's pose is always somewhat awkward as he is both emerging and kneeling at the same time.

The third character is Eve. Her head appears above Adam's, her body behind his, and her pose is ambiguous. Is she waiting her turn after Adam or already out of her sepulcher ahead of him?

The fourth and final character is Hades. *In this cosmic drama, Hades names both a person and a place, or better, a personified place that represents universal human fate.* Hades-the-Person is imagined as the ancient guardian and powerful custodian of Hades-the-Place which is, quite simply, the grave-writ-large, the prison-house of Death, as it were, where all must enter, and none can leave.

Christ's right foot tramples down the head of Hades-the-Person in the traditional sign of conquest and control. But, in futile resistance, Hades-the-Person grasps Adam's knee to pull him back into Hades-the-Place. Notice that closed circle of struggle from foot to head to arm to knee.

That scenario depicts Jesus liberating humanity from "Hades" which names both the inevitable prison-house of Death and an intractable prison-warden of Death— "Hades" as both place and person. Also, as just mentioned, the trajectory of this image will emphasize increasingly that it is Jesus as the *Crucified One* who is that *Cosmic Liberator.*

INTO CHRISTIANITY'S THIRD MILLENNIUM

When John wrote that "God so loved *the world*" (John 3:16), we know that all of us are included in that "world." But if John had said that "God so loved humanity," would we automatically think of "the world" as included? We can, for example, remember that we are made "in the image and likeness of God" (Genesis 1:26a & 1:27a) without recalling with equal emphasis that our divine "image and likeness" is immediately specified to mean our "dominion"-as-stewardship over God's just-created world (Genesis 1:26b & 1:27b).

In biblical tradition, therefore, humanity's identity and integrity is that of divine stewards for creation, humanity's destiny and authority is that of cosmic guardians of the world. Yet, all too often, we think and act not of *world-with-us* but of *us-without-world.* In this chapter, we propose a remedy against that fateful separation of us-and-world or, worse, fatal conflict of us-against-world. That remedy is to recombine the West's Individual Resurrection with the East's Universal Resurrection as the necessary Easter for Christianity's third millennium.

When Easter-West combines with Easter-East, Christ, emphasized as the Crucified One in four different ways, liberates all of humanity, embodied in Adam and Eve, from Death, symbolized as the prison-house of Hades. That liberation is not from our individual deaths, of course, but from the communal, corporate, universal death of our species as such.

Only nonviolent resistance—the vision for which Jesus lived and died—can save humanity from the escalatory violence that threatens the very sustainability of our species.

The biblical tradition knows that escalatory violence endangers both humanity and creation so that we should "not learn war any more" (Isaiah 2:4; Micah 4:3). It also knows that the socio-economic violence that targeting the vulnerable and oppressed—widows, orphans, poor people, and immigrants— "shakes the foundations of the earth" (Psalm 82:5). The hope of Easter is not to prevent the personal death that is individually inevitable but to subvert the global death that is universally predictable—by either the sudden onrush or the slow spread of escalatory-violence.

HADES, DEATH AND THE ROMAN EMPIRE

Jesus' universal resurrection represents a lifting of all humanity from the depths of Hades and the clutches of death. Such a profoundly divine and universal act, as with many of Jesus' actions and miracles, carried a radical message. Despite the savagery of Jesus' public execution on the cross after hours of relentless torture, his resurrection marked a glorious, miraculous, and rebellious triumph over the dominating power of the Roman Empire. That a poor day-laborer who led a nonviolent movement was resurrected is a sacred scandal in light of its anti-imperial message and meaning. Even after death, Jesus continued to inspire the holy and recalcitrant movement for God's Reign on Earth as a direct and nonviolent challenge to Roman imperial domination.

Jesus' vision and movement reflected God's desire for the poor, downtrodden and tyrannized to experience the fullness of life and dignity on this earth. Rather than devoured, consumed and hoarded by the mighty and powerful, the abundant resources of the earth were to be distributed justly and enjoyed communally. A life on earth rooted in God's love, abundance and justice, as Jesus modeled, is to be realized through a participatory, communal, collaborative and Spirit-rooted movement of people whose courage, love and compassion are foundational to carving a path of liberation from the death grip of Hades (corporate colonialism, authoritarianism, militarism, racism, sexism, etc.)

Jesus' lifting of humanity from the depths of death through his resurrection is a bold and resounding proclamation of the universality of this vision and message. The enduring vision of God's Reign on Earth is to be realized not through a passive religiosity, but rather through a Spirit-filled fervor and radical protagonism of the poor and exploited to collaborate *with* God in the building of God's Reign on Earth.

As depicted in the eastern Easter image of the resurrection, death does not let go easily. In Roman times, death was a gripping and brutal reality that was ever present, most especially for the masses of poor and destitute workers, day laborers, slaves, women, elderly and children. The relentless and pervasive reality of hunger, disease, poverty, exploitation and violence for the countless people who were subjected to Roman domination meant that the dark cloud of death hung over their lives constantly. Life under the crushing weight of Roman imperial rule was cruel and torturous. It is difficult to imagine such depths of unbearable suffering and pain unless one has endured war, genocide, colonial rule or enslavement.

THE UNIVERSAL RESURRECTION AS A STORY OF ANTI-IMPERIAL RESISTANCE

While the centrality of storytelling as a distinctively human practice has continued to diminish in our lifetime, stories and narratives were central to understanding all aspects of life, creation, and the divine during Jesus' lifetime. As Jesus and his disciples made their way from town to town throughout Galilee during his public ministry, stories about his encounters, miracles, and healings rapidly spread throughout the region. It was the rapid grassroots promulgation of these stories from person to person and village to village that both captivated Jesus' believers and provoked his detractors. The stories and narratives surrounding Jesus' holy and subversive Reign of God vision were spreading like an insuppressible mustard seed in a vineyard - thus making the stories and narratives themselves increasingly difficult for Rome and the high priests to quell.

Long before Jesus had been born and stories began to evolve and spread about the birth of the Messiah, the Prince of Peace and the Son of Man, the Roman Empire had developed its own grand narrative about its divine role in bringing peace to the world through victory and domination. Rome's ideological and religious propaganda was a powerful dimension to its strategic efforts to maintain its iron grip of physical, economic and psychological power over its territorial subjects.

As a countervailing force to the ideological convictions that undergird imperial domination, grand religious narratives and stories such as the story of the Exodus and God's intervention in the liberation of the Hebrew people from Egyptian bondage is a primary example of revolutionary stories that reveal God's fundamental liberatory nature. These stories and narratives are central to challenging the ideological foundations of empires and dominant systems. During Jesus' lifetime and in the period preceding his birth, the Exodus story continued to evoke and stir profound emotions that inspired both violent and nonviolent resistance throughout the many decades of Jewish struggle against Roman imperial oppression.

This is precisely why Pilate would lead extra troops to Jerusalem each Passover to demonstrate their vastly superior military capabilities and to deter any uprisings through intimidation and terror. The stories that spread throughout Galilee and beyond after Jesus' execution often brought about punishment and death for those who courageously sought to spread the message of Jesus' vision and universal resurrection. Rome rightly understood that the promulgation of the story of Jesus' resurrection, because of its life affirming and anti-imperial message, was a threat to its dominant political, economic, military, and ideological system and order.

Roman society, built upon the backs of countless enslaved, desperately poor and colonized people, rested precariously on a corrupt, volatile and violent political and economic foundation. Conversely, Jesus' universal resurrection represented a radical departure from the Roman worldview of crushing inequality and endless imperial conquest. His resurrection represented a profound cosmic revelation of a new world, here on this earth, predicated upon God's cosmic justice and distributive egalitarianism.

This vision took concrete form in the earliest Christian communities. As Acts 2:44–45 recounts, believers "had all things in common" and freely gave "to any who had need"—a revolutionary reordering of human relationships that erased economic divisions and embodied God's liberating justice in real, material terms. Tragically, the revolutionary force of Jesus' resurrection as a sign of God's cosmic justice has largely been absent from the collective consciousness of Christianity. Millions of Christians around the world are largely entrapped within cultures where capitalistic, individualistic, militaristic, and nationalistic values are the dominant norm. The revolutionary story of the resurrection remains a dormant balm of hope for Jesus' followers to claim in response to the profound challenges of the 21st century.

People's movements and grassroots revolutions require stories and grand narratives to cast a vision of hope and possibility that broadens our moral, spiritual and political imagination. That moves well beyond our current state of affairs, which grimly accepts suffering, affliction, violence and vast inequality as inevitable realities. As Nelson Mandela once said, "poverty is not an accident. It is man-made like slavery and apartheid and can be removed by the actions of human beings." Transforming societies requires both human action and conviction that is rooted in the belief that an alternative world is indeed possible. In the field of community organizing, we refer to this as the *world as we want it to be* and, for us Christians, we refer to this as God's Reign on Earth. That belief is often rooted in stories that inspire, guide and galvanize human action.

Throughout the Civil Rights movement, the moral and political struggle to dismantle Jim Crow laws and to secure equal rights for African Americans was often framed and understood in spiritual and religious terms as a 20th century freedom movement similar to the Hebrew freedom movement from Egyptian enslavement led by Moses, Aaron and Miriam. Many within the Civil Rights movement held the spiritual conviction that God was guiding and accompanying them on their perilous and holy pilgrimage through the parting seas of American racism, militarism and poverty. Much as Jewish nonviolent organizers and leaders saw their struggle against Roman imperial oppression as a continuation of God's unfolding vision, many including Dr. King, Ella Baker, and Howard Thurman saw their struggle as being both deeply spiritual and political in nature.

Although a great deal of meticulous tactical planning and remarkably high stakes grassroots strategy went into the major organizing campaigns in the south during the 1960's, it is a mistake to recognize it as simply a political movement just as it is a mistake to view Jesus' Reign of God movement as simply being a religious one. Both movements were deeply rooted in the faith traditions of their respective communities and cultures. The religious fervor and moral imagination that emerged from those movements through stories and narratives, carried profound political implications and significance.

The story of Jesus' resurrection, which rapidly spread throughout Galilee and beyond because of the courage of Mary Magdalene and the other first female apostles, ensured that his vision and movement would not die on a cross, nor in a dark cave. If the reign of the Roman Empire represented death, Jesus' counter vision of God's Reign on Earth represented life. If Rome could not kill Jesus and his movement, it meant that God could not be thwarted, silenced, or defeated. Roman power was no match for God's divine power. Death would not have the last word.

A significant theological and political aspect of Jesus' universal resurrection was its defiant challenge to the sheer psychological domination that the Roman Empire inflicted over the lives of its subjects. All political and economic aspects of life were controlled by Roman power. Movements could be crushed. Leaders could be crucified. Hope could be suffocated. Pontius Pilate and the Roman Empire, full of hubris and arrogance, believed that their execution of Jesus of Nazareth had extinguished his spirit and the flame of his movement. The miracle of the resurrection story can partly be understood as a bold and prophetic proclamation that Jesus' vision, spirit, and Reign of God movement could not be contained or shackled in Hades and by forces of death (Rome).

Jesus' movement was not solely defined by its bold and prophetic actions or by the many miraculous moments of mercy and compassion, but also by the power and influence of its grand spiritual narrative and vision, which became harder and harder, and eventually impossible, for the Roman Empire to contain and destroy. The universality of Jesus' resurrection can only be fully understood within its appropriate time and place, and yet it has transcended that particular time and place. The universal resurrection overcoming the forces of death is a potent challenge and reminder to Christians that the resurrection is not simply a singular moment in history, but a continual struggle and journey by *Resurrection People* to realize God's vision for justice on earth.

THE PRESENT-DAY RESURRECTION OVER DEATH

Jesus' first followers would have understood not only the theological significance of his resurrection, but the politically explosive essence of it as well. Roman crucifixion failed to end the Reign of God movement. Jesus' universal resurrection was a holy and defiant response to the worst of Rome's evil machinations to crush his vision and message. Tragically, this social and political context is often missing from most western theological interpretations of Jesus' resurrection. Rather than viewing Jesus' death and resurrection through an individualistic lens, a universal interpretation challenges Christians to follow the crucible path that Jesus paved. This path involves a much deeper and far more profound test of our faith, compassion and courage in seeking to overcome the forces of death that perpetuate suffering, exploitation and violence in our world today.

The path of the universal and cosmic Jesus also demands much more of us spiritually by being people who are with and for others, especially those who are the most oppressed and exploited. This requires engagement with the world and with political and economic systems that shape and determine the quality of people's lives and the long-term sustainability and survival of our planet. Pope Francis encouraged Christians to get involved in politics and to get "their hands dirty" even if the process is frustrating and fraught with failure, because politics is where we seek the common good. This stands in contrast to an individualistic interpretation of the resurrection where our primary concern lies with our own personal salvation and moral purity.

Just as first-century Christians understood the significance of Jesus' resurrection as a proclamation of life against the forces of death within their midst, what then are we to make of the theological and political significance of Jesus' cosmic and universal resurrection today? If Rome and death were inseparably equated with one another during the life and resurrection of Jesus, what are the primary purveyors of death and despair in our contemporary society and world? These are imperative questions for Christians to reflect upon.

At the 2024 Congress for the Coalition for Spiritual and Public Leadership (CSPL) where John Dominic Crossan presented a three-part lecture series on the historical Jesus, we posed this question to the gathering of grassroots Catholic and Christian leaders from across Chicago and the Midwest. As people who are trying to live out their faith in neighborhoods and communities that are far too familiar with poverty and violence, they offered a myriad of insightful reflections about what Jesus' resurrection overcoming death meant to them.

Economic exploitation in the workplace, racism and the pervasiveness of racial profiling in their neighborhoods and under-resourced schools, parks and public institutions were just a few of the examples they offered. Many of the people gathered at this event could relate to what they learned about the social, political and economic conditions that Jesus and his people faced over 2,000 years ago. They spoke of their experiences at factories in the United States that produce foods and consumer goods that are notorious for employing underage workers or harassing undocumented workers with deportation threats when they voice concerns about unsafe working conditions and wage theft.

Others spoke of the vast inequality of wealth in the country that leaves them feeling increasingly stressed and uncertain. The rising cost of food and utilities, the astronomical rise in rent and the ballooning fees for essential medical services or medicines, coupled with the diminishing purchasing power of their wages leaves millions of families desperate for economic fairness and justice. Many spoke of the manner in which the economy and political system, both domestically in the U.S. and abroad, seem to be rigged against them while being incredibly lucrative for the powerful and wealthy.

Herod Antipas and his economic system of extractive exploitation of what became Lake Tiberias, cared naught for the delicate and ancient ecosystem that was being pillaged or the humans who were being physically drained and psychologically consumed by fear and stress. For all the fish, grapes, olives, bread, and wine that the fishermen and day laborers produced, the scandal was not that there was insufficient food to go around, but that the overwhelming share of food available was vastly hoarded by the wealthy and powerful.

This was true as well during Ireland's potato famine between 1842 and 1852. While the famine was triggered by a potato disease called blight, the human catastrophe of starvation and death that ensued was largely due to British imperialism. The potatoes that did grow healthy due to the painstaking labor of Irish workers were consumed and sold by wealthy British landowners who held stolen Irish lands. Irish workers themselves were forced to work on the lands of their ancestors for extremely low wages. The famine led to the death of over 1 million Irish people and forced the migration of over 1 million more who fled the country. Jesus would have understood immediately the connection between Herod Antipas' commercialization and exploitation of the Sea of Galilee and the British Empire's theft and commercialization of Irish lands and the exploitation of its people. Likewise, millions of vulnerable people and families from Mexico, Central and South America have been forced to flee their native homelands over many decades because of the vast pillaging of their lands and natural resources by U.S. corporations as a result of exploitative and imperialistic U.S. policies.

While the economic system of the Roman Empire produced an intoxicating stream of revenue and immense wealth to fund its expansive territorial ambitions and to support the lavish lifestyles of its ruling class, it produced nothing but death and despair for those on the bottom. This barbaric form of wealth accumulation and resource extraction is not too dissimilar from the unbridled and morally corrupt capitalistic economic system that is pervasive in the United States and in markets across the world today.

The economy of the 21st century is controlled by a small and disturbingly powerful number of nations and corporations that shape and determine international affairs and economic markets. Collusion between the heads of corporations and powerful nations, which routinely leads to the structural double-dealing patterns of tax evasion, deregulation, environmental extraction, union busting and other tactics for exploiting working-class people and natural resources, is a fundamental feature of our economic system. Despite the fact that the United States is the world's richest nation, poverty remains a persistent scandal due to the dominant political and economic powers that are committed to maintaining extreme wealth inequality. At the root of the problem is the imbalance of power between the overwhelming majority of the world's people and economic and political elites.

The suffering and exploitation of millions of poor people across the world are requisite features of our current global economic system and political order. Our planet's ecosystem is rapidly destabilizing due to the environmental wreckage that has been wrought by the world's most powerful nations and corporations. During an address to leaders of popular movements in Bolivia in 2015 Pope Francis said: "Let us not be afraid to say it: we want change, real change, structural change. This system is by now intolerable: farm workers find it intolerable, laborers find it intolerable, communities find it intolerable, peoples find it intolerable... The earth itself finds it intolerable." An economy of death for so many is a system that must be changed and overcome. Jesus' universal resurrection over death calls on Christians to change the present systems that are intolerable and inhumane.

BECOMING RESURRECTION PEOPLE

The universal resurrection of Jesus continues to speak to the local and global realities and challenges of our present time. Death is tragically all around us as witnessed through the systemic and pervasive forms of violence, human exploitation and ecological degradation that persist for the sake of maximizing profits and accumulating power. The Roman Empire no longer represents death today as it did for 1st century Christians and Jews. However, there is no shortage of nation states and corporations in the 21st century that are skilled in the callous art of death-dealing. Yet for all the war, poverty, political volatility, environmental instability, there is life as well. The story of Jesus' cosmic and universal resurrection should and can be a reminder of God's enduring fidelity to the poor and oppressed in times of despair and darkness.

The meaning of Jesus' life and resurrection is a reflection of the journey that Christians are called to embark on in order to follow the path of kinship and solidarity that he walked. Christianity has unfortunately become a religion that, more often than not, is known for comforting the already comfortable, harshly judging the poor and destitute, and legitimizing hate and oppression. In the United States, as well as in countries around the world, many powerful political, economic and military figures proudly proclaim their Christian faith while endorsing war and violence and advocating for policies that dehumanize and exploit.

How have we strayed so far from the core message of love, compassion and justice that Jesus taught? How is it so many who profess to be Christians are strident supporters of Christian nationalism, white supremacy, and unfettered capitalism? For many, what comes first is culture and if culture is steeped in capitalism, nationalism, individualism, racism, sexism and militarism, it will more than likely define and shape their theological and political worldview. This is why we must root our understanding of Jesus' message as well as the deeper meaning of his resurrection within a 1st century matrix and context.

The resurrection is an invitation for Christians to follow Jesus' path by becoming a Resurrected People. What exactly do we mean when we say to become a "Resurrected Person"? It means becoming a Christian who is committed to being a protagonist for God's liberatory love, compassion, grace and justice in the world. Gustavo Gutierrez, the famous Peruvian theologian, reflected on the significance of Jesus' resurrection: "The resurrection of Jesus is the definitive manifestation of God's option for the poor. It reveals a God who is with the oppressed, and who brings new life, freedom, and hope amid the death-dealing powers of this world. To be Christians is to be resurrection people, living signs of that new life in the midst of suffering and injustice."

Our world desperately needs people who demonstrate through their love and courage new signs of life in the midst of the present suffering and injustice today. The writings and insights of theologians such as Gustavo Gutierrez and Jon Sobrino affirm that each of us is called to be a resurrected person.

To be a resurrected person involves committing oneself spiritually to a profoundly countercultural process of transformation. A commitment to nurturing both our interior and exterior life is essential. Through a sustained practice of intentional reflection, prayer, contemplation and discernment we can gradually become increasingly conscious of the ways in which the dominant culture around us shapes our beliefs, perceptions, actions and convictions. Through this process of gradual spiritual and moral maturation, and the critical development of our consciousness, we can then name and identify with moral clarity and conviction the death-dealing forces around us that cause pain and suffering in our society. Paulo Freire, the famous Brazilian educator and philosopher, speaks of this as a process of *conscientization*.

Jesus modeled a prophetic way of life that was rooted in deep prayer, discernment and compassionate encounter, which shaped his moral consciousness. He was then able to courageously demonstrate countercultural commitments, such as his willingness to embrace the leadership of women when it was shunned upon within the 1st century. There was also his desire to vulnerably accompany those who were deemed to be outcasts because of their physical condition or social status. The spiritual genius of Jesus was reflected through his openness to God's expansive grace, mercy, love and righteous desire for justice and this informed and guided his exterior commitments and actions.

It is tempting to believe that only a small number of people, perhaps priests and nuns, academic intellectuals or people in high positions are able to truly comprehend and model what it means to be a resurrected person. However, the reality is that God is calling each of us, and, most especially, the poor and marginalized, to be signs of new life and resurrected people in the world today. Perhaps there is no clearer sign of this than the way in which Jesus invited people of all walks of life, such as Bartimaeus and the woman at the well, to participate as collaborators and protagonists in the unfolding creation of the Reign of God on Earth. Jesus' life in this world was a living testament to this new way of life for those he encountered. His universal and cosmic resurrection ensured that Jesus was simply not just another revolutionary, but that the new way of life he ushered in would endure as a path for Christians to follow in seeking to overcome the forces of death in our world and journey towards the fullness of life that God intends for all of humanity and creation.

CONCLUSION

You will have already noticed in the preceding pages how regularly and deliberately we start with history before moving thence to theology and spirituality. The reason is that, for us, theology is the deepest meaning and transcendental interpretation of history and, at least on the surface, history belongs to divinity and theology to humanity. That is why and how, for us, history and theology must dance together to the music "the morning stars sing together" at the dawn, not of Civilization, but of Creation (Job 38:7).

You will also have noticed that just as you prod fire with a poker for warmth and light, we repeatedly prod history with questions to create and develop theology. So here then is a critical question: What happens when history and theology disagree, when history on our best reconstruction and theology in our best interpretation will simply not credibly or even plausibly cohere? Do we change history or change theology?

It is especially important to ask that question in our modern world of smiling lies, alternative facts, fake news, aspirations masquerading as interpretations, and conspiracy theories where truth is at best an individual opinion or, at worst, an obsolete artifact. It is necessary now more than ever to defend the very possibility of truth and call things by their proper name, be it in politics or religion, public square or church sanctuary.

Always and ever, but especially today, biblical texts are not exempt from such evaluation. Rather, since their authors invoke transcendental authority to make universal claims, they should be subject to the most careful scrutiny and critical appraisal. In this book, therefore, we began programmatically with history, moved thence to its deep interpretation in theology, and finally to its practical application in spirituality. Theology without history becomes superstition and spirituality without theology becomes sentimentality.

ON THE HISTORICAL JESUS
AND OUR PRESENT CHALLENGES

It is profoundly important that our understanding of Jesus' life, vision, execution, and resurrection, be rooted within the context of his time and place in history. This cannot be overstated. Most especially in light of the crisis that Christianity faces within our society and world. History has repeatedly shown that many who profess to be Christian are willing to bend and manipulate Jesus' message and vision to promote and advance a hateful, racist, violent, xenophobic, and ruthlessly rapacious agenda.

The tightening grip of political authoritarianism and white Christian nationalism, along with the widening gulf of income inequality in the United States in the 21st century, has been a long time in the making. Tragically, the political, economic and ideological forces behind these tectonic shifts have long been foundational flaws of the United States and have been aided and abetted by a powerful coalition of right-wing Christian figures and institutions. What has amplified the voice and influence of many key figures on the Christian right are major tech companies such as Meta and Google. These multinational corporations generate billions in profits by peddling hateful, xenophobic and conspiratorial views often produced and promoted by Christian outlets and influencers on Instagram, Facebook, YouTube, and X.

So much of what masquerades as Christianity today is rooted in lies, falsehoods, half-truths, and the dominant ideological forces that feed racism, greed, militarism, consumerism, sexism, and white Christian nationalism. Many millions of people are enamored by false prophets who espouse their love for Christ and speak of being Godly and faithful. However, their words and actions are often hollow and absent of God's love. Their public lives are animated and emboldened by spewing vitriol and sowing division, a clear sign of the presence and influence of the false spirit.

Many of these celebrity right-wing Christians have amassed millions of social media followers as a result. The more pugnacious, belligerent and polarizing their message, the more clicks and views they receive. Often their Christian takes are steeped in patriarchal, patriotic, and conspiratorial views. Rather than challenging their followers to embrace a spiritual path that is rooted in love, compassion, mercy, justice and reconciliation, their basic theological message has been adapted to fit in perfectly with the dominant cultural and ideological forces that sustain U.S. imperialism, corporate greed, and rugged individualism.

There is nothing countercultural, revolutionary or genuinely authentic to the spirit of Jesus' message and vision in much of what American Christianity represents today in the public sphere. What has emerged are theological positions and claims that are twisted and warped. Scriptural passages are taken out of context and recklessly misapplied in order to justify gun ownership, expanded militarism, and a nationalistic fervor that is idolatrous; all of which is diametrically opposed to Jesus' vision.

The prevalence of the prosperity gospel in the United States, Latin America and in other parts of the world is a painfully vivid example of a theology that is made possible, because of capitalism's overwhelming grip and intoxicating allure in our lives. Pastors jump through hoops to contend that God desires people to be wealthy, healthy, and materially prosperous. They point to suffering or poverty as a sign of a person's or family's lack of faith, while willfully ignoring the systemic structures that keep people impoverished and exploited. The inner emptiness that so many people feel and experience, cannot possibly be filled by materialistic and financial excess, but only through communities of fraternity, compassion, justice and peace that are sustained by God's love and grace.

Some may view a book that explores Jesus' life and nonviolent vision through the lens of modern 20th and 21st century organizing and liberation movements as offensive or unfaithful. Others who are less hostile to this scholarly endeavor may still consider it unnecessary. It may somehow seem incongruent with the longstanding religious traditions, practices and beliefs that they hold.

In response, we believe that genuine curiosity about the historical Jesus can coexist in deep union with many of the traditions and cultural practices which shape and inform our spiritual lives and cultural religiosity.

For example, many scholars have illuminated the remarkable theological implications of Juan Diego's encounters with the Virgen de Guadalupe by exploring Juan Diego Cuāuhtlahtoātzin's life as a Nahua peasant. The historical context of his life within the colonial period in which he lived adds remarkable depth to the story. That Mary chose to appear to a poor indigenous peasant, rather than a powerful Spanish priest or member of the ruling class, reveals a profound theological insight: God is present amongst those who are impoverished and marginalized and is a balm of courage, hope, and strength in the midst of their struggles.

Similarly, the historical Jesus can animate our faith by broadening our understanding of the meaning and significance of Jesus' words, teachings and actions within his 1st century context in such a way that illuminates the depth of his moral and spiritual wisdom far more powerfully today. The world that we live in is rife with increasingly urgent and complex social, political, economic, racial and environmental challenges. While the world that Jesus lived in 2,000 years ago was radically different from ours today, there are a great deal of similarities. Both then and now, powerful figures, institutions and empires squeeze, exploit and denigrate poor and vulnerable people, as we explored in the prior chapters.

The story of this 1st century Galilean Jew within his appropriate historical matrix of time and place holds profound insights for us in the 21st century. Rampant economic and environmental exploitation, expansive militaristic surveillance and domination, ruthless forms of imperialism and authoritarianism, dehumanizing ideological and cultural beliefs and the co-optation of religious institutions are all realities that Jesus and his people faced in one manner or another throughout his life. These are all realities that we likewise face today within our 21st century world.

Jesus' response to this was to inspire and organize a movement of poor people, women, landless workers, fisherman, and many others who were plagued with sickness and disease. Contrary to Jesus' way of love, compassion and grace, Rome and its local collaborators treated the people at the center of Jesus' Reign of God movement with disdain and viewed them as disposable and criminals. The vision and teachings that Jesus developed and proclaimed did not simply emerge from thin air. They were rooted deeply within the prophetic Hebrew tradition of which he was clearly a student.

Moses, Isaiah, Jeremiah and Job were Jesus' teachers, and he beautifully modeled a life of deep prayer, contemplation, and union with God and the Holy Spirit. With humility and grace, we also see that he learned from his experiences alongside many others throughout his public ministry. He perceived insights from the Holy Spirit in his encounters with women, children, the sick and even those who persecuted and sought to do him harm. This continually broadened and expanded his vision and teachings well beyond what was normative and culturally acceptable during his time.

With love, compassion and courage, Jesus sought to respond to God's call by traveling to and spending time with the poorest and most desperate people across 1st century Galilee and Judea. As we noted in Chapter 1, Jesus went to where the action was. He evidenced this by choosing to concentrate most of his public ministry along the Sea of Galilee as it became Lake Tiberias. He would then eventually make his way to the epicenter of political, economic and religious power in Jerusalem during Passover. What a daunting, powerful and inspiring testament of Jesus' devotion to his Reign of God vision and nonviolent movement.

As Dietrich Bonhoeffer testified throughout and at the end of his life, there is a great cost to Christian discipleship. Our hope is that this book serves as a source of inspiration for those committed not only to worshiping Jesus, but to the much more difficult task of following Jesus.

ON ORGANIZING AND HOPE

Jesus and his people had been repeatedly traumatized and brutalized. They were effectively a colonized people, with no political power or civil rights, living under a vast imperial military occupation, stripped of much of their dignity and self-worth. That a world-altering, revolutionary, nonviolent and grassroots movement emerged from such depths of despair is a testament to the spiritual and moral force of Jesus' enduring message and vision.

As we explored in the preceding chapters, Christians and people of faith have been inspired and guided by Jesus' wisdom and vision throughout history to organize powerful people's movements. These movements and struggles have been organized and led by grassroots communities. Women, students, workers and union members, Catholic sisters, pastors, grassroots faith leaders, and countless others parted the waters of oppression in their pursuit of freedom and justice. When it appeared that no path towards a more loving and humane future was possible, God's enduring love, grace and preferential option for the poor was a balm of hope and resilience. Our ancestors are beckoning us to take the risk, to embrace the uncertain path and to follow the steps of Jesus.

During his papacy, Pope Francis elevated the importance of grassroots popular movements throughout the world and within the Catholic Church. The World Meeting of Popular Movements, a Vatican-backed initiative that was started by Pope Francis, brought together grassroots organizers, young people, artisans, farmers and workers, indigenous leaders and many others whose lives have been committed to building a more just and loving world. These gatherings have signaled support from the Catholic Church for those who are organizers of hope in neighborhoods, villages, towns, cities and places where many preferred not to go. Pope Francis not only encouraged the nurturing and growth of grassroots popular movements; he also repeatedly invited Christians to get involved in politics. By encouraging us to "get our hands dirty" through direct engagement in public life and in concrete issues, Pope Francis believed that working towards addressing poverty and promoting justice was one of the most important paths to achieving the common good.

Pope Francis' papacy was a watershed moment for community organizers who have sought to engage more churches and people of faith in efforts to address the root causes of poverty, violence, political powerlessness and social disintegration. At a more fundamental level, grassroots community organizing is a practice of encountering the sacred in one another. The work of grassroots organizers and community leaders involves listening deeply and forming genuine relationships based on mutuality. Through this process of encounter and forming relationships, we seek to identify and nurture the innate leadership capacities in one another.

Each encounter, each new relationship, each grassroots protagonist who realizes their capacity and that of their community is evidence of the divine in our midst. Jesus could see the inherent dignity, gifts, talents, hopes, and dreams within those he encountered, even when they could not see this for themselves due to the weight of social, cultural, political, economic and religious pressures that had weighed down their sense of dignity and self-worth. Miracles and revolutions begin with holy encounters.

OUR RECOMMENDATIONS
Ways to Connect and Get Involved

Join a faith-based organization engaged in community organizing and justice work: We cannot possibly do the work that must be done alone. For this reason, we believe one of the most important steps you can take is to get involved with a local organization that is working for justice. Many thousands of people and their churches are engaged in the work of faith-based community organizing.

The Coalition for Spiritual and Public Leadership (CSPL) is a community organizing coalition rooted in the Catholic and Christian faith traditions. To learn more about CSPL you can visit their website at www.csplaction.org. Several national faith-based organizing networks such as Faith in Action, the Industrial Areas Foundation, Gamaliel, and DART have local affiliate organizations in cities and states across the country.

Get involved with a faith community, union or civic organization: Getting involved with a faith community, a union or a local civic organization that shares many of your values is profoundly important. Becoming a member of a congregation or organization that nurtures our spiritual lives and human connection to others is profoundly important in combating the sense of social isolation and political powerlessness that is so pervasive in our country and world.

A wonderful place we recommend for spiritual seekers who are in search of connection and deep spiritual formation is the Center for Action and Contemplation. This organization and community founded by Fr. Richard Rohr offers a myriad of rich resources for those who desire to be transformed in their interior lives and engaged in the work of social transformation. You can visit their website at www.cac.org.

Steps for Inner Fortitude and Self-awareness

Know you are a child of God: Let us remember that we are children of God. We are each created in the image and likeness of God. Furthermore, Jesus modeled for us how we are to be collaborators with God and with one another in the building of God's Reign on Earth. Each and every one of us. We were all created by God to do something important, to be peacemakers, to be bearers of compassion and mercy and to be promoters of justice. We can all make a meaningful and impactful contribution to the common good.

Know your gifts and talents: We are all born with unique gifts, talents and capacities. Some of us may not think that we have something to offer and contribute, but we all do. Failing to use our gifts in service to building a more just and loving society and world is a tragedy. One way that we discover our gifts is by reflecting on what we know we do well and what brings you and other people around you joy. This involves both reflection as well as being a part of a community. We as humans are meant to be in community with one another. To learn, grow and develop together is a fundamental part of the human experience and journey.

If you want to work for justice and engage in a good struggle, you have to know your enemy: Our present struggle is both spiritual and political. It is against the pervasive evils of greed, violence, racism, patriarchy, apathy, arrogance and the desire to dominate and subdue people, entire ethnic groups, nations and our earth. These morally and spiritually corrosive impulses are rooted in what St. Ignatius calls the false spirit. They live within each of us. They penetrate the consciousness and spirit of each person as well as the collective consciousness of nations, governments, political parties and organizations. Individuals are capable of both good and evil. Collectively, when humans act together through organizations, institutions and entities, they can perpetuate far greater good or far greater evil.

In St. Paul's letter to the Ephesians he reminds us that "we do not struggle against flesh and blood, but against the rulers, against the authorities, against the cosmic powers over this present darkness, against the spiritual forces of evil in the heavenly places" (Ephesians 6:12). In community organizing it is essential to develop and run specific, concrete and tangible grassroots organizing campaigns. Such campaigns may seek to exercise accountability, sway a decision or change an outcome involving a politician, business figure, political party, corporation or other institution. Still, our ultimate struggle is not against any single person, politician, business figure, political party, organization or corporation, but against the unjust processes they represent. The underlying political, cultural and ideological forces that have fostered vast income inequality, the entrenchment of racism and patriarchy, xenophobia, polarization, environmental degradation and disdain for the poor and working class in the United States and across the world will not disappear as a result of just one election, but as a result of many elections and changes yet to come.

Therefore, we must recognize that, while our organizing must seek to be concrete and strategic in ways to make a tangible and meaningful difference in improving people's lives, our long-term goals must also look towards the horizon beyond any single entity or person. Our struggle must also involve contending with the spiritual impulses, beliefs and convictions that are antithetical to God's will. When these spiritual impulses go unexamined and unchallenged, they develop into political, economic, ideological and military policies, systems and structures that fracture the human family, diminish human flourishing, entrap people in poverty, and lead to environmental degradation.

Fears and anxieties that lead to othering, greed, avarice, and ruthless ambition for power and control, are all impulses and convictions rooted in the evil spirit. When the evil spirit goes unchecked, when democratic political systems fail to provide checks and balances, and when the children of light fail to engage in the rough and tumble of public life that serves as a buttress against the worst impulses of the children of darkness, we enter into periods of totalitarianism, authoritarianism and vast political and economic inequality.

Balancing our spiritual wisdom with political shrewdness and acuity is essential. We must seek to better understand structures of systemic injustice; their underlying motivations and impulses, their sources of power, how they operate, who they are governed and controlled by and the layers of self-interest and interconnected relationships that drive them. This involves not only political wisdom, but spiritual wisdom as well. These and many other questions are critically important to explore, analyze, and, ultimately, to act on. May we follow the revolutionary path of the historical Jesus and continue his Reign of God movement.

ACKNOWLEDGEMENTS

We cannot conclude this book without extending our sincerest thanks to Nancy Sexton and Sarah Sexton Crossan, our patient proofreaders. We also extend our deepest gratitude to Daryl Grigsby and Joanna Arellano-Gonzalez, who served as our contributing editors. Their thoughtful feedback, patient rereading, and deep understanding of the message, purpose, and spirit we hoped to convey are invaluable. Their insight, passion and care helped bring this book to life in ways we could only have imagined.

ABOUT THE AUTHORS

John Dominic Crossan, Professor Emeritus of Religious Studies at DePaul University, Chicago, is an Irish-born biblical scholar with two-year post-doctoral diplomas in exegesis from Rome's Pontifical Biblical Institute and in archeology from Jerusalem's École Biblique. He has been a mendicant friar and a Roman Catholic priest, a Co-Chair of the Jesus Seminar, and a President of the Society of Biblical Literature. His focus, whether scholarly or popular, whether in books, videos, or lectures, is on the historical Jesus as the norm and criterion for the entire Christian Bible.

Michael Okinczyc-Cruz, Executive Director and co-founder of the Coalition for Spiritual and Public Leadership (CSPL), is a community organizer who has worked alongside faith communities and thousands of grassroots leaders to address poverty, violence and systemic inequities. He is also an adjunct associate professor at the Institute of Pastoral Studies at Loyola University Chicago. Michael possesses a BA from the University of California-Berkeley, a Master's in Theology from Colgate Rochester Crozer Divinity School and a Doctorate of Ministry from Fordham University.

Contacting the Authors: For speaking or media inquiries, please visit www.jesusandjusticebook.com.